ISBN 978-1-333-59880-8
PIBN 10524639

1 MONTH OF
FREE
READING

at
www.ForgottenBooks.com

By purchasing this book you are eligible for one month membership to ForgottenBooks.com, giving you unlimited access to our entire collection of over 700,000 titles via our web site and mobile apps.

To claim your free month visit:
www.forgottenbooks.com/free524639

RUDIMENTS

OF THE

GERMAN LANGUAGE.

EXERCISES

IN

PRONOUNCING, SPELLING, TRANSLATING,
AND GERMAN SCRIPT.

BY

Dr. F. AHN.

NEW YORK:

E. Steiger.

Wm R Hearst

1878

RUDIMENTS

OF THE

GERMAN LANGUAGE.

EXERCISES

IN

PRONOUNCING, SPELLING, TRANSLATING, AND GERMAN SCRIPT.

BY

Dr. F. AHN,

Author of the "New Method of Learning the German Language
etc. etc.

21. EDITION.
Enlarged.

NEW YORK:

E. STEIGER.

1873.

NOTICE.

These "RUDIMENTS" are compiled on the plan of AHN's larger "Method." The elements of the German language are here presented in their utmost simplicity, compactly arranged in easy gradations from the simplest forms to the more complex, the whole carefully adapted to the understanding of young pupils.

In preparing this edition, some important improvements have been introduced to lighten the difficulty of pronunciation and spelling, and to impart a *free and correct use of German Script*. Some interesting reading lessons have also been added, to engage the attention of pupils already familiar with the rudimentary parts adapted to beginners. Thus, this little work is rendered still more worthy of the high reputation it has enjoyed for many years.

Also published by E. STEIGER, and for sale by all booksellers:

F. AHN. *German Primer.* Edited by W. GRAUERT. (Printed in large type, and with much German Script.) Boards $0.35.

—— *Method of Learning the German Language.* Revised by GUSTAVUS FISCHER. (With German Script.) First Course, Boards $0.50; Second Course, Boards $0.50; Both together, Half Roan, $1.00.

—— *New Practical and Easy Method of Learning the German Language.* With Pronunciation by J. C. OEHLSCHLÆGER. (With many Reading Exercises in German Script.)
First Course (Practical Part), Boards $0.60; Second Course (Theoretical Part), Boards $0.40; Both together, Boards $1.00, Half Roan $1.25.

—— *German Handwriting.* A Companion to every German Grammar and Reader. (All in German Script.) Boards $0.40.

—— *Manual of German Conversation.* Revised by W. GRAUERT. Cloth $1.00.

Entered, according to Act of Congress, in the year 1867, by
E. Steiger,
in the Clerk's Office of the District Court of the United States for the Southern District of NEW YORK.

E. STEIGER, NEW YORK,
Printer and Electrotyper.

FIRST PART.

The German Alphabet is composed of the following twenty-six letters:

German:	English:	Name:	German:	English:	Name:
𝕬 a,	A a,	ah,	𝕹 n,	N n,	en,
𝕭 b,	B b,	bay,	𝕺 o,	O o,	o,
𝕮 c,	C c,	tsay,	𝕻 p,	P p,	pay,
𝕯 d,	D d,	day,	𝕼 q,	Q q,	koo,
𝕰 e,	E e,	ay,	𝕽 r,	R r,	err,
𝕱 f,	F f,	ef,	𝕾 ſ s,	S s,	ess,
𝕲 g,	G g,	gay,	𝕿 t,	T t,	tay,
𝕳 h,	H h,	hah,	𝖀 u,	U u,	oo,
𝕵 i,	I i,	ee,	𝖁 v,	V v,	fow (fou)
𝕵 j,	J j,	yot,	𝖂 w,	W w,	vay,
𝕶 k,	K k,	kah,	𝖃 x,	X x,	ix,
𝕷 l,	L l,	el,	𝖄 y,	Y y,	ypseelon
𝕸 m,	M m	em,	𝖅 z,	Z z,	tset.

Simple vowels: a, e, i, o, u, (y).
Modified vowels; ä, ö, ü.
Diphthongs, or compound sounds: au, ei, eu, äu, ai.
All other letters are consonants.

Pronunciation.

1.

i J, · I, n N, „ N,

m M, „ M, u U ¨ U,

i like **i** in *bit,* or **ee** in *beer.*
n and m have the same sounds as **n** and **m** in English.
u like **oo** in *roof.*

> in, ni, im, mi, mu, um, un, nu,
> ni, nim, nimm. nun, mun.

in, nun, nun, nimm.

OBSERVATION.—A double consonant is preceded by a short vowel.

2.

e E, „ e, r R, „ R, d D, ʃ, S

e like **e** in *their* or *bed,* or like **ei** in *sleigh.*
d at the beginning of a syllable like the English **d,** at the end almost like **t.**
r, unlike the English **r,** pronounced with greater force and a rolling sound.

er, der, dem, den, du, dir, mir, nur, und, rund, dumm,
irr denn, Mund. Rind, Dur, Murr, Rum.

[handwritten German cursive lines]

In final syllables **e** is very short, and must be pronounced softly:

re ben, ir ben, be nen, nen nen, mur ren, im mer, en ben, min bern, Er be, Mi ne, Mi me, Reb ner, Im me, Ru ber, Rin ne, Num mer, E ben.

[handwritten German cursive lines]

3.

o 𝔒, o 𝒪, a 𝔄, a 𝒜.

o like **o** in *not* or in *stone*.
a like **a** in *hard*, *father*.

an, ba, man, arm, o ber, mor ben, orb nen, an bre, Dorn, Monb, Ranb, Norb, Dom, Darm, Rab, A ber, Am me, Mo be, Da me, Or ben, Na me, Mar mor.

[handwritten German cursive lines]

4.

ꝟ B, w W, ꝡꝡ

ꝟ sounds like the English **f.**
w is pronounced almost like the English **v.**

von, vor, wo, wenn, wann, vorn, vom, warm, wund, wird,
wer den, we der, win den, wid men, vor dre, wan dern,
wor an, vor an, Wind, Wand, Win de, Wun der,
Wurm, Nerv, Wa de, Vor mund, Wid der, Wan ne.

[handwritten script, five lines]

5.

b B, l L, l L, l L, f F, f F.

b, l, f have the same sounds as **b, l, f** in English; **b,** at the
end of a word, is pronounced almost like **p.**

bin, ab, ob, o ben, a ber, brav, bin den, we ben, Bad,
Bo den, Brod, Band, Bir ne, Bu be, Brü der,
Ra be, Eb be.

[handwritten script, four lines]

ben, ler nen, lal len, voll, al le, rol len, lin dern,
Lob, La de, Lamm, Le der, Lar ve, Ball, Wil le.

[handwritten cursive script, several lines]

fern, fromm, fremd, fal len, of fen, ru fen, wer fen,
Feld, Far be, Fe der, Flam me, Fu der, Waf fe,
O fen, Wolf.

[handwritten cursive script, several lines]

A bend, Blu me, Dorf, El le, Fal le, Man del, Ne bel,
Re be, U fer, Waf fel.

6.

p P, *p P*, t T, *t T*

p and t have the same sounds as **p** and **t** in English.

plump, pral len, pap pen, Pal me, Pu del, Pul ver,
Pup pe, Pap pel, Map pe, Pfan ne, Pferd, Pfund, Napf,
Op fer, Dampf, Pfrop fen.

[handwritten cursive script]

[handwritten German script]

toll, tra ben, to ben, tref fen, bra ten, buf ten, ret ten,
Ta bel, Tan ne, Tob, Tritt, Luft, Va ter, Mut ter.

[handwritten German script]

tap fer, platt, Trep pe, Trop fen, Tul pe, Trumpf,
Tem pel, Pfor te.

7.

ħ. Ħ, *[handwritten: h H]*

ħ is aspirated, like **h** in the English word *hold*. After a
vowel or a **t**, ħ is not pronounced, but indicates that
the syllable is long. **pħ** is pronounced like **f.**

ħer, ħin, ħell, ħalb, ħolb, ħart, ħerb, ħel fen, ħof fen,
Ħa fer, Ħalm, Ħerr, Ħeft, Ħirt, Ħim mel, Ħof,
Ħop fen, Ħuf, Ħunb.

[handwritten German script]

weh, roh, froh, na hen, fle hen, bro hen, ruh en, Reh,
Lo he, Tru he, Le hen, E he.

hohl, lahm, wahr, ihm, ihr, mehr, ih nen, feh len,
prah len, Pfahl, Fah ne, Leh ne, Lehm, Ohr, Boh rer,
Uhr, Ruhm, thu en, roth, Thal, Thurm, Thor, Thron,
Muth, Ru the, Rath, That, Drath, Werth, Fahrt,
Phi lipp, A dolph.

8.

ä Ae,   ä̈ An,   ö Oe,   ö̈ On,

ü Ue,   ü̈ Un.

ä like **a** in *care, late.*
ö almost like **u** in *murder.*
ü has no corresponding sound in English; it is pronounced
     like the French **u**.

än bern, äh neln, wäh len, fäl len, nä hen, näh ren, nä hern,
Aeh re, Bär, Wär me, Wär ter, Thrä ne, Lärm, Thä ter.

ö de, blö de, thö nern, hö ren, öff nen, wöl ben, töb ten,
Oel, Röh re, Löf fel, Flö te, Pfört ner, Hö he, Mör der.

ü ber, für, früh, fünf, dünn, mü de, füh len, fül len,
hüp fen. Ue bel, Blü the, Müh le, Mül ler, Thür,
Mü he, Hül fe, Hüt te.

mähen, röthen, dünn, trüben

pochen, Ärmel, Ofen, Mähne,

Mörtel, Rübe, Würfel.

9.

ſ S, s,   *f T, t.*

ſ has a somewhat softer sound than the English s.
s is used at the end of words and of parts of compound
words.

ſo, ſehr, ſel ten, ſam meln, ſä en, ſe hen, ſitt ſam, Saft,
Sä bel, Sohn, Söl ler, Sumpf, Sün de, Senf, Sil ber.

le ſen, lö ſen, bla ſen, laſ ſen, eſ ſen, wiſ ſen, müſ ſen,
Ba ſe, Fa ſer, Be ſen, Fer ſe, Ro ſe, Sen ſe, In ſel,
Hül ſe, Waſ ſer, Bläſ ſe, Seſ ſel, Meſ ſer, Poſ ſe,
Rüſ ſel, Biſ ſen, Taſ ſe.

es, das, bis, was, als, uns, los, an ders, bos haft,
Hals, Fels, Wamms, Puls, Vers, Sims, Mops.

Hanft, senden, böse, fassen, öfters,

zittern, Donner, Rippe, Rose,

Lesen, Mörser, Flosse.

10.

f K, [cursive], ck, [cursive], q Q, [cursive]

f sounds like the English **k**; **ck** replaces double **k**.
q, always followed by **u**, sounds like **qu** in *quire*.

kalt, klar, krumm, kühl, knapp, kne ten, knüp fen, klop fen,
Kampf, Kä se, Korf, Kör per, Kuh, Kü fer, Keh le,
Kerl, Kind, Klet te, Klip pe, Kna be, Knall, Knopf,
Kno ten, Kro ne, Krebs.

frank, den ken, trin ken, mel ken, wel ken, mer ken, wir ken,
Ha ken, Lu fe, E kel, Dank, Wink, Volk, Wol ke, Kork,
Bir ke, Markt, Mus kel, Mas ke.

dick, keck, wa cker, tro cken, bü cken, we cken, Druck, Sack,
Pflock, Krü cke, Na cken, Bä cker, De ckel, Klecks.

quer, quitt, quä len, qua ken, be quem, Quel le, Qual,
Quit te, Qualm, Quart, Qua der.

[handwritten cursive lines]

11

sch Sch, [cursive] st St, [cursive]
sp Sp, [cursive]

sch sounds like the English **sh.**

ſt and ſp like **st** and **sp** in English, at the beginning of a
word approaching the sound **sht** and **shp**

ſcharf, ſchön, ſchlimm, ſchmal, ſchnell, ſchroff, ſchwer, ſchwül,
Sche mel, Schiff, Schuh, Schlaf, Schlit ten, Schmuck,
Schua bel, Schreck, Schrift, Schwan, Schwur, Schwert,
raſch, friſch, barſch, falſch, hübſch, fi ſchen, quet ſchen,
Tiſch, Buſch, Froſch, Menſch, Hirſch, Wunſch, Fla ſche,
Wä ſche, Kut ſche.

faſt, erſt, wüſt, dü ſter, fonſt, ge ſtern, hu ſten, flü ſtern,
liſ peln, haſ peln, Aſt, Bruſt, Pflaſter, Qua ſte, Ki ſte,
Kü ſte, Froſt, Forſt, Schwe ſter, Bür ſte, Obſt, Papſt,
Pol ſter, Kunſt, Ham ſter, Knoſ pe, Weſ pe.

ſtark, ſtill, ſtumm, ſtö ren, ſteh len, ſtol pern, ſtri cken, Stahl,
Stern, Stock, Stu be, Strahl, Strand, Stroh, Strumpf.

ſpa ren, ſpät, ſpin nen, ſpü len, ſprö de, ſprü hen, ſproſ ſen,
S eck, Spott, Sporn, Spund, Spal te, Spin del, Split ter.

12.

ch, ⸝ſ.

ch, in the middle or at the end of a word, has two different
sounds. For the correct pronunciation the pupil must
refer to his teacher, as there is no corresponding sound
in English.

ich, mich, nicht, durch, recht, ſchlecht, wel cher, man cher,
rä chen, ſpre chen, fürch ten, hor chen, ſchnar chen, rech nen,
Strich, Blech, Kelch, Milch, Dolch, Mönch, Storch, Knecht,
Pflicht, Rich ter, Kü che, Kö cher, Fä cher, Ler che, Kir che,
Fur che, Mäd chen, Hüt chen.

nach, wach, noch, hoch, ſacht, ma chen, ko chen, ſu chen,
ſchlach ten, Bach, Schmach, Tuch, Bruch, Loch, Nacht,
Docht, Schlucht, Sa che, Spra che, Wo che, Bu che,
Toch ter, Sta chel, Na chen, Kno chen.

chs or chſ is pronounced like x when these consonants belong
to the root or radical syllable.

ſechs, wach ſen, wich ſen, drech ſeln, wech ſeln, Lachs,
Dachs, Wachs, Fuchs, Ochs, Ach ſe, Büch ſe, Ach ſel.

13.

g G, *y G.*

g, at the beginning of a word, sounds like the English **g** in
good; between two vowels, and at the end of a syllable,
the sound is generally like **ch,** only much softened.

gar, gut, gelb, grün, glatt, grob, ge ſtern, ge ra de,
Ga bel, Gans, Geld, Gicht, Glas, Glo cke, Gna de,
Gras, Gur ke.

arg, ſchräg, ge gen, trä ge, reg nen, ſeg nen, mö gen,
lü gen, ar tig, e wig, rich tig, tüch tig, Weg, Steg,
Talg, Sarg, Berg, Burg, Ge gend, Ke gel, Sä ge,
Flü gel, Igel, Bür ger, Or gel, Gur gel, Kö nig,
Ho nig.

flug, flugs, ge nug, ma ger, ſa gen, fra gen, kla gen,
Tag, Trog, Flug, Pflug, Magd, La ger, Na gel, Pla ge,
Bo gen, Wo ge, Vo gel, Rog gen, Flag ge.

ng sounds like **ng** in *ring.* The pronunciation is the same,
when **ng** is followed by a vowel, like *fing-er,* not like
the English *fin-ger.*

eng, ſtreng, längſt, ge ring, ban ge, brin gen, ſin gen,
ſpren gen, Gang, Klang, Ding, Ring, Schwung, En gel,
Wan ge, Fin ger, Angſt, Hengſt.

gern, karg, wenig, mächtig,
drängen, ſchlagen, Gaſt, Glück.

[handwritten:] Gipfel, Lyzeum, Rettig, Wagner
Schwager Kranz, Mängel

14.

ß, *ß.*

ß is either preceded by a long vowel and has the sound óf the English **ss**, or is used instead of **ſß** at the end of a word, and of **ff** before **t**.

groß, bloß, ſüß, Fuß, Gruß, Ruß, Maß, Spaß, Stoß, Kloß, Stra ße, Bu ße, Mu ße, Grö ße.

daß, naß, blaß, Schuß, Nuß, Roß, Schloß, Faß, Haß, Riß, Biß, Schluß, Fluß, Kuß, Gäßchen, miß lich, ge wiß, ge faßt, be wußt.

[handwritten:] Floß Fraß, Troß, Laß
mäßig, faßlich

15.

j J, *j J,* z 3, *z Z,* ß, *tz.*
x X, *x X.*

j is pronounced like **y** in *you*.
z sounds like **ts**; **ß** replaces double **z**.
x sounds like **x**.

ja, je, jäh, jeder, jung, jüngſt, jedoch, Jagd, Jäger,
Jahr, Joch, Jubel, Jugend, Juwel.

zu, zäh, zahm, zehn, zwar, zwölf, zwiſchen, Zahn,
Zehe, Zeche, Zoll, Zunge, Zucker, Zimmer, Zwang,
Zwerg, kurz, ſchwarz, ſtolz, ganz, zwanzig, krächzen,
ſchluchzen, Schwanz, Pflanze, Schmalz, Pelz, Holz,
Harz, Schmerz, Kerze, Schürze.

trotz, ſpitz, jetzt, zuletzt, ſetzen, ſchätzen, putzen, ſchützen,
Satz, Netz, Blitz, Klotz, Katze, Fetzen, Nutzen, Spritze,
Mütze.

fix, Art, Knix, Hexe, Examen, Exempel, Xerxes.

16.

au, au, äu, äu, eu, eu, ai, ai.

au is pronounced like **ou** in *house*, *out*.
äu and **eu** sound almost like **oy** in *boy*.
ai is pronounced by drawing the sounds of **a** and **i** quickly
together.

aus, auf, auch, grau, blau, rauh, laut, taugen, tauchen,

Frau, Thau, Braut, Haus, Haupt, Strauch, Faust,
Strauß, Baum, Zaun, Staub, Au ge, Schnau ze,
Dau men, Pau ke.

räu men, träu men, räu chern, täu schen, gläu big, gräu=
lich, Säu le, Räu ber, Käu fer, Bäum chen, Mäus chen,
Käuz chen.

neu, euch, neun, treu, the u er, eu er, heut, beu ten,
beu gen, Heu, Kreuz, Zeug, Freund, Feu er, Freu de,
Heuch ler, Leuch ter, Scheu ne.

Mai, Mais, Lai e, Wai se, Kai ser, Sai te.

17.

ei, ~; ie, ~.

ei sounds like **i** in *side*.
ie sounds like **ie** in *field*, or **ee** in *beer*.

ein, zwei, drei, nein, mein, dein, fein, klein, frei, heim,
heil, weit, breit, feig, reich, leicht, weiß, Ei, Eis, Kreis,
Beil, Zeit, Wein, Weib, Zweig, Teich, Reiz, Geiz,
Kleid, Fleiß, Geist, Reif, Keim, Rei he, Klei e, Zwei fel,
Ei che, Gei ge, Fräu lein.

die, wie, nie, viel, vier, sie ben, tief, wie der, lieb, nie der,
frie ren, flie ßen, krie chen, lie gen, flie hen, Dieb, Thier,

Knie, Vieh, Krieg, Kies, Spieß, Bier, Spiel, Dienst, Pfriem, Glied, Bie ne, Zie ge, Rie men, Stie fel, Prie ster.

[handwritten cursive text]

sei, sie, zei hen, zie hen, sie den, sei den, ver schei den, ver schie den, rei chen, rie chen, Lied, Leid, Kiel, Keil, Reis, Ries, Fließ, Fleiß, Rie se, Rei se, Wei se, Wie se.

18.

aa, *aa,* **ee,** *ee,* **oo,** *oo.*

aa, ee, oo sound like **a, e, o,** and are always long.

baar, Paar, Haar, Saal, Saat, Schaar, Waa re.

leer, scheel, Schnee, Klee, Beet, Heer, Bee re, See le.

Moor, Boot, Loos, Schooß.

[handwritten cursive text]

19.

y Y, y N, c C, L, Ch, Ch,

ti, ti,

in words derived from foreign languages.

y is pronounced like **i.**

Ly risch, my thisch, Hy ä ne, Ty rann, Syl phe, Sym bol,
Py ra mi de, Phy sik, Nym phe, Hym ne.

c is pronounced like **z** before **ä, e, ö, i, y,** and like **k** before
a, o, u, or a consonant.

Cä sar, Ce der, Cent ner, Ci ster ne, Ci tro ne, Cy pref se,
Ca pi tal, Cla vier, Com mo de, Com paß, Con greß,
Con cert.

ch is pronounced before **ä, e, i, y** like **ch** in **ich,** before other
vowels or consonants, in general, like **k.** In words
derived from the French, it sounds almost like **sh.**

Che mie, Che rub, Chi rurg.
Cha os, Cha rak ter, Chor, Christ.
Char pie, Cho co la de, Cham pag ner.

The syllable **ti,** when followed by a vowel, is generally pronounced like **zi.**

Na ti on, Por ti on, Auc ti on. Pa ti ent, Ac ti e.

Mythe, System, Cylinder,
Lypin, Corsar, Choral, Lution.

THE SYLLABIC ACCENT.

SIMPLE WORDS.

Simple words have the accent, in general, on the root or radical syllable.

They are either monosyllabic roots, or consist of the root and one or more unaccented syllables. The latter may be placed *before* the root, as **be, emp, ent, er, ge, ver, zer,** or *after* the root, as **e, el, en, end, er, ern, es, est, et, icht, ig, in, isch, lich, chen, ung.**

EXAMPLES.

auf, an, bei, durch, gut, arm, groß, klein, Frau, Kind,
Haus, Dach.

Be ruf', Em pfang', Ent wurf', Er trag', Ge sang',
Ver nunft', Zer fall'

Er'de, Vo'gel, Be'sen, Tu'gend, wie'der, zau'bern, al'les,
Kö'nig, Dick'icht, kin'disch, Lö'win, kind'lich, Mäd'chen,
Woh'nung.

in'ner lich, öf'fent lich, ju'gend lich, wäs'se rig, we'nig stens,
ü'bri gens, eu'bi gen, schwär'me risch, Kö'ni gin, Müt'ter=
chen, Rei'sen der, Wit'te rung.

ent beh'ren, zer trüm'mern, em pfind'lich, em pö'rend, ge=
wal'tig, er in'ner lich, ver ei'ni gen, ver deut'li chen, be stä'ti=
gen, Ge bir'ge, Ent deck'er, Be er'di gung, Ver wun'de rung,
Er man'ge lung.

Many words taken from foreign languages, have the accent on the last syllable.

EXAMPLES.

Stu dent', Pa pier', Sol dat', Ma jor', Ge ne ral', Ka meel',
Mo rast', Con cert', Mu sik', Na tur', E rem plar',
Ter min', fa tal'.

COMPOUND WORDS.

Compound words are either combinations of independent words, or may partly consist of accented prefixes, as **un, miß,** or of accented final syllables, as **bar, haft, ling, sal, schaft, niß, rich, sam, thum, lein, ei, heit, keit, iren.**

Each component keeps its proper accent, the principal accent being, in general, laid on the first component.

EXAMPLES.

vor'nehm, an'ge nehm, mit'lei dig, ü'ber mü thig, um'kommen, auf'hö ren, ein'neh men, ent ge'gen ge hen, An'fang, Ant'wort, Her'kunft, Nach'richt, Durch'schnitt, Vor'mund, Wi'der spruch, Ue'ber zug, Aus'sa ge, Auf'wär ter, Ge'gen ge schenk, Hin'ter ge bäu de, Vor'be deu tung.

blaß'grün, geist'reich, him'mel blau, hart'her zig, bau'fäl lig, lie'bens wür dig, to'des mu thig, wohl'ge bo ren, Haus'thür, Land'mann, Froh'sinn, Mein'eid, Sand'wü ste, Druck'feh ler, Roth'kehl chen, Schlaf'zim mer, Mei'ster stück, A'ber glau be, Blu'men gar ten, Re'gen was ser, Ge bet' buch, Ge burts'tag, Schieß'ge wehr, Sil'ber ge schirr, Men' schen ver stand, Rei'se ge fähr te, Maul'beer baum, Ur'groß mut ter.

furcht'bar, bos'haft, mu'ster haft, be hut'sam, un'ar tig, un'frucht bar, un'be dacht sam, miß'ge stal tet, Lieb'ling, Schick'sal, Freund'schaft, Hei'math, Fräu'lein, Fin'ster niß, Ver säum'niß, Frei'heit, Wü'the rich, Für'sten thum, Fein'heit, Un'glück, Miß'wachs, Miß'ge schick, Ent schlos'sen heit, Un'dank bar keit, Jüng'lings al ter.

There are, however, a number of compoúnd words which have the principal accent not on the first component.

EXAMPLES.

bar an', zu rück', zu wi'ber, vor her', wo von', hin ein', her ab', an bei', burch aus', in bef'fen, ü ber haupt', berg= auf', ge gen ü'ber.

all mä'lig, vor han'ben, zu künf'tig, barm her'zig, all mäch'= tig, vor treff'lich, un fehl'bar.

voll en'ben, miß lin'gen, burch blät'tern, um ar'men, ü ber= tref'fen, hin ter ge'hen, wi ber fpre'chen, un ter fu'chen.

fpa zie'ren, re gie'ren, ftu bi'ren, mar fchi'ren, buch fta bi'ren.

Prah le rei', Ein fie be lei', Vier tel jahr', Jahr hun'bert, Son nen auf'gang.

SECOND PART.

—

PRACTICAL EXERCISES.

1.

ber (masc.), bie (fem.), baß (neut.), the.

ber Vater, the father.	ber Garten, the garden.
bie Mutter, the mother.	bie Stabt, the town, the city.
baß Buch, the book.	baß Meſſer, the knife.

unb, and.

OBSERVATION.—1) All German nouns begin with a capital letter.
2) Articles, adjectives and pronouns must, in general, be repeated before each noun to which they belong.

EXAMPLE.—The father and mother. Der Vater unb bie Mutter.

Der Vater unb bie Mutter. Der Garten unb bie Stabt. Das Buch unb baß Meſſer.

2.

ber Sohn, the son.	ber Tiſch, the table.
bie Tochter, the daughter.	bie Feber, the pen.
baß Haus, the house.	baß Papier, the paper.

Der Sohn unb bie Tochter. Die Feber unb baß Papier. Der Tiſch unb baß Haus. Der Vater unb ber Sohn. Die Mutter unb bie Tochter. Das Buch unb bie Feber. Das Haus unb ber Garten.

21

3.

der Mann, the man.	der Hund, the dog.
die Frau, the woman.	die Katze, the cat.
das Kind, the child.	das Pferd, the horse.

Der Mann, die Frau, das Kind. Der Hund, die Katze und das Pferd. Der Vater, die Mutter und das Kind. Das Buch, die Feder und das Papier. Das Haus, der Garten und die Stadt. Der Tisch, das Messer und die Feder.

4.

der Bruder, the brother.	der Vogel, the bird.
die Schwester, the sister.	die Blume, the flower.
das Dorf, the village.	das Schloß, the castle.

Der Bruder und die Schwester. Der Vogel und die Blume. Das Dorf und das Schloß. Der Vater und der Bruder. Die Mutter und die Schwester. Das Dorf und die Stadt. Der Mann und das Kind. Die Frau und die Tochter. Der Tisch und das Messer.

5.

The father and the mother. The son and the daughter. The brother and the sister. The man and the woman. The house and the garden. The dog and the cat. The pen and the knife. The village and the castle. The bird and the flower. The book and the child. The dog and the horse.

6.

ein (masc.), eine (fem.), ein (neut.), a, an.

ein Vater, a father; eine Mutter, a mother; ein Buch, a book.

Ein Vater und eine Mutter. Ein Sohn und eine Tochter. Ein Bruder und eine Schwester. Ein Mann und eine Frau. Ein Garten, eine Stadt und ein Haus. Ein Buch und eine Feder. Ein Hund, eine Katze und ein Pferd. Ein Dorf und ein Schloß.

7.

Ein Vogel und eine Blume. Ein Dorf und eine Stadt. Eine Feder und ein Papier. Ein Buch und ein Messer. Ein Vater und ein Kind. Ein Tisch und ein Haus. Eine Tochter und eine Schwester. Ein Sohn und ein Bruder.

8.

A man and a woman. A cat and a dog. A horse and a bird. A town and a village. A father and a child. A mother and a daughter. A knife and a pen. A book and a flower. A table and a pen. A brother and a sister. A son and a daughter. A garden and a house.

9.

mein, meine, mein, **my.**

dein, deine, dein, **your (thy).**

der Onkel, the uncle.	der Freund, the friend.
die Tante, the aunt.	die Flasche, the bottle.
das Glas, the glass.	das Wasser, the water.

Mein Onkel und meine Tante. Mein Glas und meine Flasche. Dein Vater und deine Mutter. Dein Bruder und deine Schwester. Mein Sohn und meine Tochter. Mein Buch und meine Feder. Dein Garten und dein Haus. Dein Hund und dein Pferd. Mein Feund und dein Freund. Meine Blume und deine Blume. Mein Messer und dein Messer.

10.

unser, unsere, unser, **our.**

euer, euere, euer, **your.**

unser Vater, our father;   unsere Mutter, our mother;

unser Haus, our house.

dein Vater, \
euer Vater, } your father.   deine Mutter, \
euere Mutter, } your mother.

dein Haus, \
euer Haus, } your house.

OBSERVATION.—*Your* is translated by dein, deine, dein, when referring to one person. It is, in the following exercises, marked *your* (1), to be distinguished from *your*, euer, euere, euer, which refers to several persons.

Unser Vater und unsere Mutter. Unser Bruder und unsere Schwester. Euer Onkel und euere Tante. Euer Sohn und euere Tochter. Unser Hund, unsere Katze und unſer Pferd. Unſere Stadt und unſer Haus. Unſer Glas und uuſere Flaſche. Unſer Kind und euer Kind. Unſer Buch und euer Buch. Unſere Feder und euere Feder. Unſer Garten und euer Garten. Unſere Blume und euere Blume. Unſer Freund und euer Freund.

11.

The uncle and the aunt. The bottle and the glass. The bottle and the water. My father and my mother. Our brother and our sister. My bird and my flower. Our garden and our house. Your town and your village. My horse and my cat. Our town and our castle. The brother and the sister. My book and my pen. Your son and your daughter. My friend and your [1] friend. My glass and my bottle. Your dog and your cat.

12

dieſer, dieſe, dieſes, this.

dieſer Vater, this father;   dieſe Mutter, this mother; dieſes Kind, this child.

Dieſer Vater, dieſe Mutter und dieſes Kind. Dieſer Garten, dieſe Stadt und dieſes Haus. Dieſes Dorf und dieſes Schloß. Dieſes Glas und dieſe Flaſche. Dieſer Mann und dieſe Frau. Dieſe Feder, dieſes Meſſer und dieſes Papier. Dieſer Hund, dieſe Katze und dieſes Pferd.

Dieſer Vogel und dieſe Blume. Dieſer Tiſch, dieſe Flaſche und dieſes Waſſer. Dieſes Buch und dieſe Feder.

13.

This horse and this dog. This dog and this ·at. This bottle and this water. This brother and ,his sister. This son and this daughter. This paper and this ·pen. This castle and this house. This father and this child. This knife and this table. This bird and this cat. This man and this woman. This town and this village.

14.

alt, old.
jung, young.
neu, new.
gut, good.
treu, faithful.
müde, tired.
Karl, Charles.

groß, great, large, tall.
klein, little, small, short.
ſchön, beautiful, fine.
krank, ill, sick.
nützlich, useful.
fleißig, diligent.
Louiſe, Louisa.

iſt, is.

Der Vater iſt alt. Die Mutter iſt jung. Das Buch ị neu. Der Garten iſt groß. Die Stadt iſt klein. Das Haus iſt ſchön. Der Hund iſt treu. Das Pferd iſt nützlich. Karl iſt fleißig. Louiſe iſt müde. Der Vogel iſt klein. Die Blume iſt ſchön. Das Dorf iſt groß. Der Onkel iſt krank. Die Tante iſt müde.

Der Tisch ist neu. Die Feder ist klein. Das Papier ist gut. Das Messer ist schön.

15.

My father is old. My mother is young. Our garden is small. Our town is large. Your horse is beautiful. Your dog is faithful. My bird is small. My son is ill. My daughter is diligent. Our table is new. Your pen is good. This book is useful. Your [1] uncle is tall. Your [1] aunt is short. My brother is tired. Charles is my brother. Louisa is my sister.

16.

nicht, not.
reich, rich; arm, poor; für, for.

Unser Vater ist nicht alt. Unsere Mutter ist nicht krank. Euer Onkel ist nicht reich. Euere Tante ist nicht arm. Mein Bruder ist nicht klein. Meine Schwester ist nicht groß. Dieses Haus ist nicht neu. Diese Blume ist nicht schön. Karl ist nicht fleißig. Louise ist nicht müde. Dein Messer ist gut. Deine Feder ist nicht gut. Mein Onkel ist krank. Meine Tante ist nicht krank. Dieser Vogel ist für Karl. Diese Blume ist für Louise.

17.

sind, are.

Mein Vater und meine Mutter sind krank. Mein Bruder und meine Schwester sind müde. Mein Buch und meine Feder sind gut. Euer Hund ist treu. Ein Hund und ein Pferd sind nützlich. Dein Vogel und deine Blume sind schön. Unser Dorf und unser Schloß sind klein. Dieser Mann und diese Frau sind alt. Unser Bruder und unsere Schwester sind jung. Diese Feder und dieses Papier sind gut. Unser Onkel und unsere Taute sind reich. Euer Sohn und euere Tochter sind fleißig.

18.

The man is not old. The woman is not young. The uncle is not rich. The aunt is not poor. This bird is not beautiful. This flower is not fine. My brother is not short. My sister is not tall. My child is not ill. Your brother is not diligent. This dog is not faithful. Charles is not my brother. Louisa is not my sister. This knife is not new. Our uncle and aunt are not young. My brother and sister are not ill. Charles and Louisa are not diligent This horse and this dog are useful. This bird and this flower are for Charles. This paper and this pen are for Louisa

19.

art'g, good, gentle.   glücklich, happy.

Ist dein Vater krank? Ist deine Mutter jung? Ist dieser Hund treu? Ist dieses Pferd nicht nützlich? Ist Karl fleißig? Ist Louise nicht ärtig? Ist diese Stadt groß? Ist dieses Dorf klein? Ist das Schloß schön? Ist euer Onkel reich? Ist euere Tante arm? Ist dieses Buch neu? Ist diese Frau nicht glücklich? Ist dieser Mann nicht fleißig?

20.

der Arzt, the physician.   Heinrich, Henry.
die Magd, the maid-servant.   Emilie, Emily.
Herr, gentleman, sir.
Hier ist, here is; da ist, there is; wo, where?

Heinrich ist mein Bruder. Emilie ist meine Schwester. Dieser Herr ist unser Arzt. Diese Frau ist unsere Magd. Karl ist mein Sohn. Louise ist meine Tochter. Hier ist euer Messer und euere Feder. Da ist dein Buch und dein Papier. Wo ist mein Onkel und meine Tante? Wo ist das Glas und die Flasche? Wo ist der Vogel und die Blume? Ist euere Magd krank? Unsere Magd ist nicht krank. Ist Heinrich müde? Heinrich ist nicht müde.

21.

Is your [1] brother ill? Is your [1] mother young? Is our physician old? Is our maid-servant faithful? Is my garden large? Is your house small? Is this gentleman your uncle? Is this dog not useful? Is this pen not good? Where is my knife? Where is my glass? Here is your [1] knife and there is your [1] glass. Is Henry not diligent? Is Emily not good? Is Charles your [1] brother? Is Louisa your [1] sister?

22.

ich bin, I am;
du bist, you are (thou art).
der Neffe, the nephew.　　munter, gay.
die Nichte, the niece.　　zufrieden, contented.
immer, always; sehr, very; ja, yes; nein, no.

Ich bin zufrieden. Du bist nicht immer zufrieden. Karl ist immer munter. Louise ist nicht immer fleißig. Ich bin dein Bruder. Du bist meine Schwester. Heinrich ist unser Freund. Bin ich glücklich? Bin ich nicht groß? Bist du krank? Bist du nicht artig? Ist Emilie nicht zufrieden? Ist dieser Herr ein Arzt? Ja, dieser Herr ist ein Arzt. Ist diese Frau euere Magd? Nein, diese Frau ist nicht unsere Magd. Ist dieses Schloß nicht schön? Ist diese Feder nicht gut? Ich bin dein Onkel, du bist mein Neffe. Bist du meine Tante? Bin ich deine Nichte? Bist du mein Freund, Heinrich? Ja, ich bin dein Freund.

23.

I am poor. You are rich. I am your [1] son, you are my father. Louisa is your [1] daughter. Henry is our friend. Are you contented, Charles? Yes, I am contented. Are you ill, Emily? No, I am not ill. You are not always diligent, Emily. Are you tired? No, I am not tired. My nephew and niece are very young. Am I your [1] friend, Henry? Yes, you are my friend. Am I not happy? Yes, you are very happy.

24.

er, ſie, es iſt, he, she, it is.

traurig, sad; aber, but; auch, also; hier, here; da, there.

Der Garten iſt nicht groß, aber er iſt ſehr ſchön. Die Stadt iſt ſchön, aber ſie iſt ſehr klein. Das Haus iſt alt; es iſt nicht neu. Mein Vater iſt krank; er iſt ſehr traurig. Iſt deine Mutter auch krauk? Nein, ſie iſt nicht krank. Iſt dieſer Hund treu? Ja, er iſt ſehr treu. Iſt dieſes Buch nicht ſchön? Ja, es iſt ſchön, aber es iſt nicht nützlich. Wo iſt Karl? Er iſt hier, Mutter. Wo iſt Emilie? Sie iſt auch hier. Iſt euer Onkel reich? Ja, er iſt ſehr reich. Iſt dieſe Frau arm? Ja, ſie iſt ſehr arm. Iſt dieſes Kind krank? Ja, es iſt ſehr krank.

25.

Is Henry your [(1)] brother? Yes, he is my brother. Is Louisa your [(1)] sister? No, she is not my sister. Is this man poor? Yes, he is very poor. Is this woman ill? No, she is not ill. · Is not our dog faithful? Yes, he is very faithful, but he is not beautiful. Is not this village small? Yes, it is very small. Is not our garden large? Yes, it is very large. Is this flower not beautiful? Yes, it is very beautiful. Is my book not useful? Yes, it is very useful. ·Where is your [(1)] brother? He is here. And your [(1)] sister? She is ill.

26.

wir ſind, we are.
ihr ſeid, you are.
ſie ſind, they are.
oder, or ;   noch, still.

OBSERVATION.—*You are*, when referring to one person, du biſt, will hereafter be marked *you* (1) *are*.

Sind wir reich oder arm? Wir ſind nicht reich. Seid ihr fleißig? Ja, Mutter, wir ſind ſehr fleißig. Sind dein Vater und deine Mutter alt? Nein, ſie ſind noch jung. Iſt der Garten und das Haus groß? Ja, ſehr groß. Sind wir artig, Mutter? Ja, ihr ſeid ſehr artig. Sind Karl und Louiſe hier? Nein, ſie ſind nicht hier. Seid ihr zufrieden? Ja, wir ſind zufrieden und glücklich. Dieſer Mann und dieſe Frau ſind ſehr arm. Wir ſind nicht arm. Wo iſt mein Buch und meine Feder? Hier iſt dein Buch, und da iſt auch deine Feder.

27.

We are happy. We are not sad. You are contented, but you are not always diligent. My father and mother are still young. Your uncle and aunt are very rich. This man and this woman are not poor. Are we rich? Are you poor? Henry and Charles are very diligent. Louisa and Emily are ill. This horse and this dog are useful. There are my book and knife. Are they good? No, they are not good.

28.

der gute Vater, the good father;
die gute Mutter, the good mother;
das gute Kind, the good child.
geſchickt, skillful; falſch, false.

OBSERVATION.—Adjectives, when preceded by the definite article der, die, das, have the termination **e**.

Der reiche Onkel. Die reiche Tante. Das ſchöne Haus. Der arme Mann. Die arme Frau. Das arme Kind. Der kleine Bruder. Die kleine Schweſter.

Das kleine Buch. Der treue Hund. Die falsche Katze. Das nützliche Pferd. Der große Garten. Die schöne Blume. Das alte Schloß. (Der) gute Heinrich. (Die) gute Emilie. Die fleißige Magd. Der geschickte Arzt. Der kleine Tisch. Der schöne Vogel.

29.

OBSERVATION.—Adjectives have the same termination e, when preceded by dieſer, dieſe, dieſes.

Dieſer gute Vater. Dieſe gute Mutter. Dieſes gute Kind. Dieſer arme Mann. Dieſe arme Frau. Dieſes arme Kind. Dieſer schöne Garten. Dieſe schöne Stadt. Dieſes schöne Dorf. Dieſer kleine Tisch. Dieſer treue Hund und dieſe falsche Katze. Dieſes alte Haus. Dieſes junge Pferd. Dieſe alte Magd. Dieſes neue Buch. Dieſer geschickte Arzt. Dieſes artige Kind. Dieſe reiche Stadt.

30.

blind, blind.

(Der) kleine Karl ist immer traurig. (Die) kleine Louiſe ist immer munter. Der gute Onkel und die gute Tante sind sehr glücklich. Der treue Hund ist nützlich. Dieſer arme Mann ist blind. Dieſe arme Frau ist krank. Dieſes kleine Kind ist sehr artig und fleißig. Dieſer reiche Mann ist ein Arzt. Dieſe schöne Frau ist unſere Tante. Dieſes nützliche Buch ist nicht neu.

Dieſer junge Mann iſt unſer Neffe. Dieſes muntere Kind iſt unſer Bruder.

31.

The good brother and the good sister. The old uncle and the old aunt. The small garden and the small house. The fine village and the fine town. The poor mother and the poor child. The blind man and the blind woman. This beautiful bird and this beautiful flower This useful book and this good paper. This good son and this good daughter. This large glass and this small bottle. This new knife and this new table. This young mother and this young child.

32.

ſcharf, sharp; lieb, dear.

OBSERVATION.—Adjectives, preceded by the indefinite article ein, eine, ein, have the terminations er (masc.), e (fem.), es (neut.).

Ein guter Mann, eine gute Mutter, ein gutes Kind. Ein reicher Onkel, eine reiche Tante. Ein treuer Hund und ein nützliches Pferd. Ein fleißiger Sohn und eine fleißige Tochter. Ein ſchönes Dorf, eine große Stadt, ein kleines Schloß. Eine treue Magd. Ein geschickter Arzt. Ein kleiner Vogel, eine ſchöne Blume, ein ſcharfes Meſſer. Ein lieber Bruder und eine liebe Schweſter.

33.

der Gärtner, the gardener; ſchon, already.

OBSERVATION.—Adjectives take the same terminations (er, e, es) when preceded by mein, dein, unſer, euer.

Mein kleiner Bruder und meine kleine Schweſter ſind artig. Dein guter Onkel und deine gute Taute ſind ſchon hier. Unſer alter Gärtner iſt blind. Euere neue Magd iſt ſehr fleißig. Biſt du ſchou müde, mein liebes Kind? Nein, Vater, ich bin nicht müde. Wo iſt dein kleiner Hund, Karl? Mein kleiner Hund iſt hier. Iſt dein junger Freund nicht ein geſchickter Arzt? Ja, er iſt ſehr geſchickt. Unſer großer Garten, unſere kleine Stadt und unſer ſchönes Haus.

34.

A little brother and a little sister. A dear uncle and a dear aunt. A rich man and a rich woman. A large town and a large village. A fine garden and a fine castle. A false cat and a faithful dog. My good father and my good mother. Your [1] little nephew and your [1] little niece. Our old gardener and our old maid-servant. Your fine garden and your fine house. Our dear brother and our dear sister. Our good paper and our good pen.

35.

der erſte, the first.	der ſiebente, the seventh.
der zweite, the second	der achte, the eighth.
der dritte, the third.	der neunte, the ninth.
der vierte, the fourth.	der zehnte, the tenth.
der fünfte, the fifth.	der elfte, the eleventh.
der ſechste, the sixth.	der zwölfte, the twelfth.

der letzte, the last.

Juni, June.	Wilhelm, William.
Juli, July.	Paul, Paul.
Auguſt, August.	Franz, Francis.
Ludwig, Lewis.	Katharine, Catherine.

Pauline, Pauline.

beſcheiden, modest.	heute, to-day.
unartig, naughty.	morgen, to-morrow.

übermorgen, the day after to-morrow.

der erſte Auguſt, the first *of* August; der vierte Juli, the fourth *of* July.

Heute iſt der ſechste Auguſt, morgen iſt der ſiebente, und übermorgen iſt der achte. Unſer lieber Karl iſt ſehr fleißig; er iſt der erſte in der Claſſe (in the class)· Ludwig iſt der zweite, Wilhelm der dritte, und (der) unartige Paul iſt der letzte. Unſere Louiſe iſt auch ein ſehr fleißiges Kind; ſie iſt nicht die letzte in der Claſſe; Emilie iſt die letzte. Papa, iſt heute der zehnte Juni? Nein, mein Lieber, heute iſt der zwölfte Juli. Franz der Erſte. Heinrich der Vierte. Karl der Fünfte.

36.

Are you [1] the first in the class, Charles? No, (Sir,) I am not the first, but I am the second

My brother is the third, Henry is the fourth, and
(the) little Lewis is the last. My sister Louisa is
very diligent; she is the first in the class; Emily
is the fifth, and Pauline is the sixth. Is not to-day
the eleventh, papa? No, my dear, to-day is the
tenth. Charles the First, William the Fourth, Henry
the Eighth, Catherine the Second.

37.

klein, small; kleiner, smaller.
alt, old; älter, older.
groß, large; größer, larger.
nützlich, useful; nützlicher, more useful.

die Erde, the earth.   der Rhein, the Rhine.
die Sonne, the sun.   die Donau, the Danube.
stark, strong; breit, broad; als, than.

OBSERVATION.—Most adjectives of one syllable change in the
comparative the vowel **a** into **ä**, **o** into **ö**, **u** into **ü**.

Ich bin kleiner, als du. Du bist größer, als ich.
Mein Vater ist älter, als meine Mutter. Meine Mutter
ist jünger, als mein Vater. Der Hund ist treuer, als
die Katze. Das Pferd ist schöner und nützlicher, als
der Hund. Wir sind zufriedener, als ihr. Ihr seid
reicher, als wir. Bist du stärker, als dein Bruder, Karl?
Nein, ich bin nicht stärker, als er. Ist Louise artiger,
als Emilie? Nein, sie ist nicht artiger. Ist diese Frau
ärmer, als unsere Magd? Ja, sie ist ärmer. Ist der

Rhein größer und breiter, als die Donau? Nein, er ist nicht größer und breiter. Ist die Erde kleiner, als die Sonne? Ja, sie ist kleiner.

38.

My brother is older than I. I am younger than he. Charles is more diligent than Lewis. This horse is more useful than that dog. Emily is more contented than Louisa. We are richer than you. You are poorer than we. The Danube is larger than the Rhine. The sun is larger than the earth. Henry is stronger than William. Are we richer than this gentleman? No, we are not richer, but we are happier.

39.

der meinige, mine;   der unsrige, ours;
der deinige, yours (thine).   der eurige, yours.
der Ring, the ring; die Uhr, the watch; das ist, that is.
nicht so....als, not so....as; so....wie, as....as.

Das ist nicht dein Ring, Karl; das ist der meinige. Das ist nicht deine Uhr, das ist die meinige. Das ist nicht dein Messer, das ist das meinige. Mein Hut ist schöner, als der deinige. Meine Schwester ist jünger, als die deinige. Unser Haus ist so groß, wie das eurige, aber euer Garten ist nicht so groß, als der unsrige. Euer Pferd ist älter, als das unsrige. Mein Buch ist nützlicher, als das deinige. Euere Magd ist nicht so fleißig, als die unsrige. Mein Onkel und der deinige sind hier. Meine Taute und die deinige sind sehr glücklich. Euer Schloß ist so schön, wie das unsrige.

40.

Your [1] hat is smaller than mine. Your [1] watch is finer than mine. My brother is older than yours [1]. My sister is not so old as yours [1]. My paper is finer than yours. [1] Our uncle is richer than yours. Our house is larger than yours. Your son is happier than ours. Your daughter is more diligent than ours. Your child is stronger than ours. Is that your [1] book, William? No, it is not mine. Is that your [1] watch? Yes, it is mine.

41.

klein, small; kleiner, smaller; der kleinste, the smallest.

alt, old; älter, older; der älteste, the oldest.

groß, large; größer, larger; der größte, the largest.

nützlich, useful; nützlicher, more useful; der nützlichste, the most useful.

das Metall, the metal.	Mathilde, Mathilda.
das Eisen, the iron.	Elise, Eliza.
das Silber, the silver.	die Aufgabe, the exercise.
das Thier, the animal.	leicht, easy.
Friedrich, Frederic.	unglücklich, unhappy.

OBSERVATION.—The superlative has the termination ste or ste. As in the comparative, most adjectives of one syllable modify the vowels a. o u into ä, ö, ü.

Heinrich ist kleiner, als Karl, aber Paul ist der kleinste. Louise ist größer, als Emilie, aber Mathilde ist die größte. (Das) Eisen ist nützlicher, als (das) Silber; es ist das nützlichste Metall. Der Hund ist das treueste Thier. Diese Aufgabe ist leichter, als die deinige, aber die eurige ist die leichteste. Karl ist mein ältester Sohn, und Louise ist meine jüngste Tochter. Du bist fleißig, aber dein Bruder ist noch fleißiger; Friedrich ist der fleißigste. Elise ist unser schönstes Kind. Wilhelm ist euer treuester Freund. Der reichste Mann ist nicht immer der zufriedenste. Der ärmste Mann ist nicht immer der unglücklichste.

42.

Frederic is more diligent than Charles, but Henry is the most diligent. Louisa is younger than Emily, but Mathilda is the youngest. This poor man is happier than your [1] rich friend. (The) iron is the most useful metal. William is stronger than Paul, but Lewis is the strongest. Your town is more beautiful than ours. Your garden is larger than ours, but this garden is the largest. Your house is smaller than this house, but ours is the smallest.

43.

sein, seine, sein, his.
ihr, ihre, ihr, her.
die Dame, the lady. die Freundin, the friend (female).
der Kutscher, the coachman.

Der Vater und sein Sohn. Der Vater und seine Tochter. Die Mutter und ihr Sohn. Unser Onkel und sein Bruder. Unser Onkel und seine Schwester. Die Tante und ihr kleiner Neffe. Die Tante und ihre kleine Nichte. Karl und sein junger Freund. Louise und ihre junge Freundin. Dieser Herr und sein neuer Kutscher. Diese Dame und ihre alte Magd. Mein Freund ist traurig; sein jüngster Bruder ist sehr krank. Meine Freundin ist sehr glücklich; ihr ältester Bruder und ihre jüngste Schwester sind hier.

44.

My uncle and his son. My uncle and his daughter. My aunt and her brother. My aunt and her sister. This gentleman and his nephew. This gentleman and his niece. This lady and her coachman. This lady and her maid-servant. This woman and her little child. Charles and his old father. Charles and his good mother. Emily and her rich uncle. Emily and her blind aunt. Mathilda is very sad; her father and mother are sick

45.

Singular.	Plural.
der Tisch, the table;	die Tische, the tables.
der Stuhl, the chair;	die Stühle, the chairs.
die Stadt, the town;	die Städte, the towns.

die Nacht, the night. die Hand, the hand.
der Hut, the hat, bonnet. der Zahn, the tooth.
der Strumpf, the stocking. der Fuß, the foot.
der Brief, the letter. der Schuh, the shoe.
die Maus, the mouse.

OBSERVATION.—Many nouns of one syllable take in the plural the termination e, and change a, o, u, au into ä, ö, ü, äu.

Das Pferd, die Pferde. Der Sohn, die Söhne. Der Freund, die Freunde. Die Nacht, die Nächte. Der Hut, die Hüte. Die Hand, die Hände. Der Zahn, die Zähne. Der Strumpf, die Strümpfe. Der Fuß, die Füße. Der Brief, die Briefe. Der Ring, die Ringe. Die Magd, die Mägde. Der Arzt, die Aerzte. Die Maus, die Mäuse. — Der Schuh, die Schuhe. Der Hund, die Hunde.

46.

kurz, short. gestern, yesterday.
rein, clean. jetzt, now.
weiß, white. Paris, Paris.
warm, warm. London, London.
das sind, these are.

OBSERVATION.—The determinative adjectives dieser, mein, dein, sein, unser &c. have in the plural the termination e: diese, meine, unsere &c.

Unsere Söhne sind sehr fleißig. Unsere Mägde sind krank. Diese Tische sind sehr klein. (Das) Eisen und (das) Silber sind Metalle. Paris und London sind Städte. (Die) Pferde sind nützlicher, als (die) Hunde. Die Nächte sind jetzt sehr kurz. Euere Hüte stud sehr groß. Karl, deine Hände sind nicht rein. Louise, deine Zähne sind nicht weiß. Sind das deine Strümpfe, Mathilde? Nein, Mutter, das sind nicht meine Strümpfe. Friedrich, sind das deine Schuhe? Nein, Mutter, das sind nicht meine Schuhe. Meine Hände und Füße sind sehr warm. Wo sind meine Ringe und meine Briefe? Hier sind deine Ringe, und da sind auch deine Briefe.

47.

Charles and Henry are my friends. Horses and dogs are useful. Frederic, there are your [1] stockings and shoes. Where are our hats and rings? Your letters are not here. My sons are ill. These towns are very large and beautiful. The nights are still very short. My hands and feet are very cold. Your maid-servants are young, but your gardener and your coachman are very old.

48.

das Kleid, the dress, the gown.	das Schloß, the castle.
das Band, the ribbon.	das Dorf, the village.
das Glas, the glass.	das Loch, the hole.
das Haus, the house.	das Blatt, the leaf.
das Buch, the book.	der Wurm, the worm.
das Kind, the child.	der Wald, the forest, the wood.
das Ei, the egg.	der Mann, the man.

OBSERVATION.—A number of monosyllabic nouns form the plural by adding er, modifying a, o, u, au into ä, ö, ü, äu.

Das Kleid, die Kleider. Das Band, die Bänder. Das Glas, die Gläser. Das Haus, die Häuser. Das Buch, die Bücher. Das Kind, die Kinder. Das Schloß, die Schlösser. Das Dorf, die Dörfer. Das Blatt, die Blätter. Der Wurm, die Würmer. Der Wald, die Wälder. Der Mann, die Männer. Das Ei, die Eier. Das Loch, die Löcher.

49.

hoch, high.	verwelkt, withered.
schmutzig, dirty.	grün, green.
häßlich, ugly.	nicht mehr, no more.

alle, all; noch nicht, not yet.

Meine Bücher sind sehr nützlich. Unsere Kinder sind krank. Deine Kleider sind schmutzig, Emilie. Alle diese Gläser sind nicht rein. Diese Dörfer sind sehr groß. Diese Schlösser sind sehr schön. Diese Bänder sind für Mathilde. Die Wälder sind nicht mehr grün. Alle Blätter sind schon verwelkt. Alle diese Häuser sind hoch. Diese Männer sind sehr stark. (Die) Würmer sind häßlich.

50.

My ribbons are very fine. Our children are very diligent. Your dresses are not dirty. These glasses are not clean. These leaves are already withered. These men are stronger than we. All worms are ugly. These houses are not high. The

woods are not yet green. These books are very
useful. All these villages are very beautiful.

51.

der Schneider, the tailor.
der Schuhmacher, the shoemaker.
der Italiener, the Italian.
der Engländer, the Englishman.
das Fenster, the window.
das Zimmer, the room.

der Spiegel, the mirror.
der Stiefel, the boot.
der Löffel, the spoon.
die Gabel, the fork.
die Nadel, the needle.
das Mädchen, the girl.

faul, lazy; zu, too.

OBSERVATION.—Masculine and neuter nouns ending in **er, el, en**
have, generally, the same termination in the plural, some changing the
radical vowels **a, o, u** into **ä, ö, ü.**

Feminine nouns ending in **er, el** take **n** in the plural, except
Mutter, Mütter; Tochter, Töchter.

Meine Brüder sind alle krank. Meine Schwestern
sind alle fleißig. Diese Löffel sind nicht rein. Diese
Messer und Gabeln sind auch nicht rein. Wo sind meine
Bücher und meine Federn? Wo sind meine Schuhe und
meine Stiefel? Unsere Schneider und Schuhmacher sind
arm. Euere Tante und ihre Töchter sind hier. Diese
Mütter sind sehr traurig; ihre Kinder sind krank. Diese
Häuser und diese Gärten sind sehr schön. Sind das deine
Nadeln, Louise? Nein, das sind nicht meine Nadeln.
Sind diese Männer Italiener? Nein, es (they) sind
Engländer. Diese Mädchen sind sehr artig. Euere Zim-
mer sind sehr schön, aber die Fenster sind zu hoch.

52.

Your sons and daughters are very happy. Our fathers and mothers are contented. These Italians and Englishmen are very rich. Where are our spoons and forks? Here are your spoons and forks, and there are also your knives. These needles are very good. Your [1] pens are too small. Charles, your [1] boots and shoes are very dirty. Your rooms are always clean. My brothers and sisters are ill. These girls are not ugly.

53.

der Löwe, the lion.	der Russe, the Russian.
der Hase, the hare.	der Franzose, the Frenchman.
die Ratte, the rat.	der Deutsche, the German.
der Knabe, the boy.	der Preuße, the Prussian.
die Kirche, the church.	die Pflaume, the plum.
die Schule, the school.	die Straße, the street.

der Apfel, the apple; der Tiger, the tiger; furchtsam, timid, afraid; liebenswürdig, amiable; tapfer, brave; besser, better.

OBSERVATION.—Nouns ending in e take n in the plural. The pronouns der meinige, unsrige &c. follow the same rule.

(Die) Löwen sind sehr stark. (Die) Löwen sind stärker, als (die) Tiger. (Die) Hasen sind sehr furchtsam. (Die) Katzen sind falsch. (Die) Mäuse sind kleiner, als (die) Ratten. Die Franzosen sind liebenswürdiger, als die Russen. Die Preußen sind sehr tapfer. Die Deutschen sind treu und fleißig. Diese Knaben und diese Mädchen find sehr munter. Meine Blumen sind schöner, als die deinigen. Deine Aufgaben sind leichter, als die meinigen. Unsere Kirchen sind größer, als die eurigen. Euere Schulen sind besser, als die unsrigen. Diese Straßen sind sehr breit, breiter, als die unsrigen. Hier sind Pflaumen für Emilie, und da sind Aepfel für Mathilde.

54.

(The) rats are larger than (the) mice. (The) dogs are more useful than (the) cats. (The) tigers are not so strong as (the) lions. These boys are mv brothers. These girls are my sisters. The Germans and the French are brave. My flowers are not so beautiful as yours [1]. Your [1] books are better than mine. These are not your hats, they (es) are ours. These are not our stockings, they are yours. Your [1] friends and mine are Germans. Your [1] sisters are more amiable than ours. Our exercises are as easy as yours.

55.

die Stunde, the hour.　　die Kirsche, the cherry.
die Schwalbe, the swallow.　angenehm, pleasant, agreeable.

OBSERVATION.—Adjectives, preceded by the definite article, or by dieser, mein, dein, sein &c. take n or en in the plural.

Die reichen Freunde. Die großen Städte. Die kleinen Dörfer. Die angenehmen Stunden. Die schöner

Häuſer. Meine guten Söhne und Töchter. Deine guten
Onkel und Tanten. Unſere fleißigen Mägde. Euere
ſchönen Kirchen und Schulen. Die breiten Straßen.
Die furchtſamen Haſen. Die falſchen Katzen. Die
treuen Hunde. Dieſe großen Spiegel. Dieſe nützlichen
Bücher. Dieſe kranken Kinder. Meine neuen Kleider.
Deine alten Stiefel. Dieſe munteren Knaben. Die
erſten Schwalben. Die letzten Kirſchen.

56.

die Ente, the duck.	die Roſe, the rose.
die Gans, the goose.	die Tulpe, the tulip.
die Frucht, the fruit.	Herr N., Mr. N.

OBSERVATION.—When the adjective is not preceded by any de
terminative word, it takes e in the plural.

(Die) Enten und Gänſe ſind große Vögel. (Die) Löwen
und Tiger ſind ſtarke Thiere. (Die) Würmer ſind häß-
liche Thiere. Paris und London ſind ſchöne Städte.
Heinrich und Karl ſind treue Freunde. Louiſe und
Mathilde ſind liebenswürdige Mädchen. Euere Söhne
und Töchter ſind fleißige Kinder. Eiſen und Silber
ſind nützliche Metalle. Kirſchen und Pflaumen ſind
angenehme Früchte. Ludwig und Wilhelm ſind muntere Knaben. Herr N. und Herr S. ſind geſchickte Aerzte.
(Die) Roſen und Tulpen ſind ſchöne Blumen.

57.

(The) dogs are faithful animals. (The) horses are useful animals. Henry and Lewis· are good children. Charles and William are naughty boys. Paris and London are large cities. The good fathers and the good mothers. My little brothers and my little sisters. These beautiful castles and gardens. The large towns and the large streets. The brave Germans and the amiable French. The skillful physicians. The poor tailors. White teeth and warm hands. The modest girls. The lazy children.

58.

ich habe, I have;	wir haben, we have;
du haſt, you have (thou hast);	ihr habt, you have;
er hat, he has;	ſie haben, they have.

die Dinte, the ink.

OBSERVATION.—The accusative of fem. and neut. nouns is like the nominative.

Ich habe das Buch. Du haſt die Feder. Karl hat die; Dinte. Franz hat das Meſſer. Wir haben das Pferd. Ihr habt die Katze. Meine Brüder haben die Tulpe und die Roſe. Ich habe ein Buch. Du haſt eine Feder. Emilie hat eine Gabel. Wilhelm hat ein Pferd. Wir haben eine Schweſter. Habt ihr ein Haus? Ich habe dein Buch. Du haſt meine Feder. Louiſe hat deine Dinte. Franz hat mein Meſſer. Wir haben euer Pferd.

Ihr habt unsere Katze. Ich habe ein gutes Buch. Du hast eine gute Feder. Karl hat immer gute Dinte. Wir haben eine gute Mutter und eine reiche Tante. Ihr habt ein schönes Schloß. Heinrich 'hat eine schöne Blume. Sophie hat eine bescheidene Schwester.

59.

I have not the knife,
I have not got the knife, } ich habe das Messer nicht.

I have a needle. You [1] have a pen. Emily has a knife. We have a cat. You have a horse. My brothers have a rose and a tulip. I have not the fork. You [1] have not the knife. Lewis has not got the ink. We have not the pen. You have not got the book. My sisters have not got the cat. Have you [1] a sister, Henry? Yes, I have a good sister. Has Emily a good mother? Yes, she has a very good mother. William has a fine flower. This gentleman has a beautiful castle.

60.

der Dichter, the poet.   der Nachbar, the neighbor.
der Künstler, the artist.   berühmt, famous.
    viel, much; viele, many; wer? who?

OBSERVATION.—The accusative plural of all nouns is like the nominative plural.

Ich habe Pferde und Hunde. Du hast die Enten und die Gänse. Ludwig hat Kirschen und Pflaumen. Wir haben die Hüte und die Bänder. Ihr habt die Löffel und die Gabeln. Meine Schweftern haben die Gläfer und die Flafchen. Wer hat meine Schuhe und meine Stiefel? Haft du meine Bücher und meine Federn? Hat Louife deine Nadeln? Unfer Onkel hat fchöne Häufer und Gärten. Ihr habt fleißige Söhne und Töchter. Die Franzofen haben gefchickte Aerzte. Die Deutfchen haben große Dichter. Haben die Engländer berühmte Künftler? Unfer Nachbar hat viele Kinder. Haft du noch viele Vögel und Blumen? Hat Heinrich noch viele Freunde? Emilie hat kleine Hände und weiße Zähne. Paris und London haben fchöne Straßen.

61.

neither... nor, weder...noch.

I have neither the bread nor the meat, ich habe weder das Brod noch das Fleifch.

I have the roses and (the) tulips. You [1] have the spoons and forks. Lewis has the knives. We have ducks and geese. You have horses and dogs. Henry and William have the flowers and fruits. I have not your [1] books. You [1] have not got my pens. We have neither the bottles nor the glasses. You have neither our hats nor our ribbons. These boys have neither the apples nor the plums.

62.

gekauft, bought	verloren, lost.
verkauft, sold.	gefunden, found.
gesehen, seen.	genommen, taken.
warum, why?	

OBSERVATION.—The past participle is detached from the auxiliary and placed at the end of the sentence.

Ich habe das Dorf und die Stadt gesehen. Hast du die Feder und das Papier genommen? Unser Onkel hat sein Haus und sein Pferd verkauft. Karl hat seine Uhr verloren. Mathilde hat ihre Freundin verloren. Wir haben ein schönes Buch gekauft. Habt ihr diese Messer und Gabeln gekauft? Wo habt ihr das Glas und die Flasche gefunden? Wer hat meine Dinte genommen? Ich habe deine Dinte nicht genommen. Warum hat euer Onkel dieses schöne Schloß nicht gekauft? Hast du meine Tante und meine Schwester nicht gesehen? Nein, ich habe weder deine Tante noch deine Schwester gesehen.

63.

I have lost my book and pen. Charles, have you [1] found my book? No, I have not found your [1] book. Where is my needle? Louisa, have you [1] taken my needle? No, I have not taken your [1] needle. Emily has lost her mother; she is very unhappy. Why have you sold your horse?

We have not sold our horse. Has your uncle bought this beautiful castle? Yes, my dear. Where have you bought this fine paper and these good pens? Henry and Lewis have not yet seen our town. My uncle has sold all his birds and flowers; we have also sold ours.

64.

ber feinige, his.

ber ihrige, hers.

gefucht, looked for; hübfch, pretty.

Hat Karl meine Feber, ober bie feinige genommen? Hat Heinrich mein Meffer, ober bas feinige genommen? Mathilbe hat meine Uhr unb bie ihrige verloren. Emilie hat mein Kleib unb bas ihrige gefucht. Wir haben euere Freunbe unb bie unfrigen gefehen. Ich habe meine Bücher unb bie beinigen gefunben. Wer hat alle biefe Löffel unb Gabeln gekauft? Unfer Gärtner hat alle feine Blumen verkauft. Diefe Bänber find hübfcher, als bie beinigen. Deine Rofen find hübfcher, als bie unfrigen. Unfere Brüber find älter, als bie eurigen. Euere Schweftern find jünger, als bie unfrigen.

65.

Henry has lost my book and his. Louisa has lost my knife and pens. William has found my pen and his. Mathilda has found my stockings and hers.

Charles has looked for your [1] watch and his. Mathilda has looked for our sister and hers. My flowers are prettier than yours [1]. Your [1] ribbons are prettier than mine. Our houses are larger than yours, but your gardens are more beautiful than ours. Are your sisters older than ours? No, they are not older.

66.

1 eins.	11 elf.
2 zwei.	12 zwölf.
3 drei.	13 dreizehn.
4 vier.	14 vierzehn.
5 fünf.	15 fünfzehn.
6 sechs.	16 sechzehn.
7 sieben.	17 siebzehn.
8 acht.	18 achtzehn.
9 neun.	19 neunzehn.
10 zehn.	20 zwanzig.

das Jahr, the year.	die Woche, the week.
der Monat, the month.	der Tag, the day.

wie alt, how old?

Unser Nachbar hat fünf Kinder, drei Söhne und zwei Töchter. Das Jahr hat zwölf Monate. Der Monat hat vier Wochen. Die Woche hat sieben Tage. Wie alt bist du? Ich bin acht Jahre alt. Meine Schwester ist zehn Jahre alt. Wir haben zwei Pferde, drei Katzen und vier Hunde. Karl hat drei Schwestern und vier Brüder. Mein Vater hat zwölf Federn und drei Messer gekauft.

Wir haben zwei Hände und zwei Füße. Unser Gärtner hat sechs Stühle gekauft.

67.

How old are you [1], my dear? I am seven years old. My little sister is not yet six years old. Is your [1] father old? No, my father is not old. My mother is still younger 'than he. Our uncle has many children; he has five sons and four daughters. We have bought fifteen ducks and twelve geese. Our gardener has sold sixteen tulips and twenty roses. Charles has taken a knife, two forks and three spoons.

68.

Nominative.	Accusative.
der Vater,	den Vater, the father.
dieser Mann,	diesen Mann, this man.

erhalten, received.	der Stock, the stick, the cane.
geschrieben, written.	der König, the king.
gelesen, read.	die Königin, the queen.

oft, often.

OBSERVATION.—Determinative words preceding a masculine noun in the accusative singular have the termination en.

Ich habe den König und die Königin gesehen. Hast du den Brief und das Buch erhalten? Mein Vater hat den Garten und das Haus verkauft. Friedrich hat den Stock und die Uhr verloren. Emilie hat den Ring nicht

gefunden. Wer hat diesen Hund und diese Katze gekauft?
Ich habe diesen Mann und diese Frau oft gesehen. Wo
habt ihr diesen schönen Spiegel gekauft? Habt ihr schon
den Rhein und die Donau gesehen? Wo hat Heinrich
diesen Tisch und diesen Stuhl genommen? Wer hat
diesen Brief geschrieben? Wer hat diesen Hut verloren?

69.

Nominative.	Accusative.
ein Garten,	einen Garten, a garden.
mein Hund,	meinen Hund, my dog.

Ich habe einen Brief erhalten. Wir haben einen
schönen Garten und ein schönes Haus gesehen. Habt ihr
schon einen Tiger gesehen? Wer hat meine Gabel und
meinen Löffel genommen? Hast du deinen Hund und
deinen Vogel verkauft? Wilhelm hat seinen Stock und
seine Uhr verloren. Mathilde hat ihren Ring noch nicht
gefunden. Diese arme Frau hat alle ihre Kinder verloren.
Deine Tante hat meinen Brief nicht gelesen. Ihr seid
glückliche Kinder; ihr habt einen guten Vater und eine
gute Mutter. Wir sind auch glücklich; wir haben einen
reichen Onkel und eine reiche Tante. Emilie ist ein hüb=
sches Mädchen; sie hat eine kleine Hand und einen kleinen
Fuß. Wir haben unseren Freund Friedrich verloren.
Habt ihr eueren Bruder und euere Schwester gefunden?
Nein, wir haben unseren Bruder und unsere Schwester
nicht gefunden.

70.

der Schreiner, the joiner; die Birne, the pear; gebracht, brought.

I have written a letter to-day. Have you [1] read my letter, Emily? No, I have not read your [1] letter. I have lost a shoe, and my brother has lost a boot. Our joiner has brought a table and a chair. I have seen your [1] little brother and your [1] little sister. We have a very skillful physician. Charles and Lewis have received a pretty ring and a beautiful watch. Mr. Smith has brought this stick for Lewis. William has lost his friend. We have lost our uncle and aunt. My mother has lost her brother and sister. Where have you found this apple and this pear? Have you already seen the king? No, we have not yet seen the king, but we have seen the queen.

71.

das Glück, the happiness, the
   good luck.
das Unglück, the misfortune.
das Vergnügen, the pleasure.

das Geschäft, the business.
das Vermögen, the fortune.
ehemals, formerly.
gehabt, had.

gemacht, made, done.

Ich habe einen guten Freund gehabt. Du hast immer gute Freunde gehabt. Karl hat meinen Stock gehabt. Ich habe deinen Ring und deine Uhr nicht gehabt. Habt ihr viel Vergnügen gehabt, Kinder? Ja, Mutter, wir

haben viel Vergnügen gehabt. Diese Kinder haben viel
Unglück gehabt; sie haben ihren Vater und ihre Mutter
verloren. Unser Nachbar hat dieses Jahr viele Pflaumen
und Kirschen gehabt. Wir haben diese Woche zehn Briefe
erhalten. Dieser Herr hat ein großes Vermögen gehabt;
er hat alle seine Häuser und Gärten verkauft und ist jetzt
ein armer Mann.

72.

beschäftigt, busy, occupied.

I have had good luck; I have found a watch and
a ring. Charles has had much pleasure; he has
seen his father and mother. Who has had my hat
and cane? Henry has had your [1] hat, and Lewis
has had your [1] cane. Have you had many apples
and pears this year? Yes, my dear, we have had
many apples and pears. My brothers have always
had good friends. We have received many letters
to-day; we are very busy.

73.

gewesen, been.   angekommen, arrived.
ausgegangen, gone out.
ich bin gewesen, I have been.
er ist angekommen, he has arrived.
sie sind ausgegangen, they have gone out.
ganz, whole, all; den ganzen Tag, the whole day, all day
wie lange, how long?   in, in.
Frau N., Mrs. N.   bei Frau N., at Mrs. N.'s

Ich bin die ganze Woche krank gewesen. Du bist immer mein Freund gewesen. Wilhelm ist hier gewesen. Wir sind immer zufrieden gewesen. Wo seid ihr gewesen? Meine Brüder sind nicht ausgegangen; sie sind den ganzen Tag sehr beschäftigt gewesen. Friedrich und Ludwig sind in Paris und London gewesen. Ihr seid in Berlin gewesen; habt ihr auch den König gesehen? Ja, wir haben den König und die Königin gesehen. Wer ist heute hier gewesen? Herr Peters ist angekommen; er hat ein Buch für Heinrich gebracht. Karl, du bist nicht fleißig gewesen; du hast deine Aufgaben noch nicht gemacht. Ich bin bei Frau Röder gewesen; sie ist eine sehr liebenswürdige Frau. Wie lange bist du in Madrid gewesen? Ich bin drei Monate da gewesen.

74.

Kopfweh, headache; der Strauß, the nosegay, the bouquet.

Are you [1] ill, Henry? Yes, I have had (a) headache all day. Where is your [1] brother? He has gone out; he has been very busy to-day. Has he already been in Versailles? No, he has not yet been there. We have been at Mrs. Bender's; she is a very good lady. How long have you been in London? We have been there four weeks. Who has been here? Our gardener has been here; he has brought a pretty nosegay for Mathilda.

Have you been diligent, children? Yes, father, we have been very diligent.

75.

m.   f.   n.

Nominative: ber, bie, baß, the.

Dative: bem, ber, bem, to the.

ber Bater, the father;   bie Mutter, the mother;

bem Bater, to the father.   ber Mutter, to the mother.

baß Kinb, the child;

bem Kinbe, to the child.

eß gehört, it belongs.   geliehen, lent.

fie gehören, they belong.   gegeben, given.

verfprochen, promised.   gezeigt, shown.

OBSERVATION.—1) biefer is declined like the definite article. 2) Most masc. and neut. nouns of one syllable take e in the dative singular. 3) The dative generally precedes the accusative.

Diefer Hut gehört bem Gärtner. Diefeß Meffer gehört ber Magb. Diefeß fchöne Hauß gehört bem Arzte. Diefer große Hunb gehört bem Nachbar. Ich habe bem Onkel unb ber Tante gefchrieben. Wir haben bem Kinbe einen Bogel verfprochen. Wer hat biefem Kinbe einen Apfel gegeben? Ich habe biefem Manne unb biefer Frau unfern Garten gezeigt. Wir haben biefer Dame ein Buch geliehen. Wir haben biefem Mäbchen einen hüb=fchen Strauß gegeben. Unfer Bater hat bem Nachbar ein Pferb verkauft. Karl hat biefem Engländer alle feine Bögel verkauft.

76.

der Fingerhut, the thimble.   der Regenschirm, the umbrella.
der Thaler, the (German) dollar.

OBSERVATION.—ein, mein, dein, &c. have in the dative singular the same terminations as the definite article: einem, einer, einem &c.

Dieses Schloß gehört einem Italiener. Diese Bücher gehören meinem Bruder. Diese Strümpfe gehören meiner Schwester. Ich habe deinem Freunde eine Feder geliehen. Mein Onkel hat unserem Nachbar ein Pferd verkauft. Louise hat ihrer Freundin einen Fingerhut geliehen. Karl hat seinem Onkel einen Brief geschrieben. Wir haben unserer Tante einen hübschen Strauß gegeben. Ihr habt euerer Magd drei Thaler gegeben. Wer hat unserer Mutter den schönen Ring verkauft? Wer hat euerer Tochter die hübschen Bänder gegeben? Wer hat deinem Freunde diesen Stock geliehen?

77.

das Brot, the bread; gebet, give.

OBSERVATION.—Adjectives preceded by one of the determinative words der, dieser, ein, mein &c. have in the dative the termination en.

Gebet diesem kleinen Mädchen eine hübsche Blume. Ich habe unserer alten Magd ein neues Kleid gegeben. Wir haben unserem lieben Onkel einen Brief geschrieben. Karl hat diesem armen Manne das Brot gegeben. Emilie hat ihrer guten Mutter einen hübschen Strauß gegeben. Wir haben deinem kleinen Bruder einen Stock geliehen.

Meine Mutter hat deiner kleinen Schwester ein hübsches Band versprochen. Mein Vater hat euerem reichen Nachbar ein Pferd verkauft. Frau Röber hat der kleinen Louise eine Uhr gegeben. Wir haben diesem armen Kinde ein Buch geliehen. Dieses Messer gehört dem alten Gärtner. Diese Nadeln gehören der kleinen Emilie.

78.
wem, to whom?

This beautiful castle belongs to the king. This fine horse belongs to the queen. To whom have you [1] given your [1] bread, Charles? I have given my bread to this poor man. To whom have you [1] lent your [1] umbrella? I have lent my umbrella to this old lady. To whom has your brother sold all his flowers? He has sold all his flowers to a rich Englishman. To whom have you shown our garden? We have shown our garden to our neighbor. Have you written a letter to your physician? Yes, we have written a letter to our physician. Henry has promised a new book to his brother. Emily has given a pretty ribbon to her sister.

79.

Nominative: der, die, das, the.
Genitive: des, der, des, of the.

der Vater, the father;   die Mutter, the mother;
des Vaters, of the father.   der Mutter, of the mother.

das Kind, the child;

des Kindes, of the child.

die Nachbarin, the neighbor (female); der Palast, the palace.

OBSERVATION.—Most masc. and neut. nouns take s or es in the genitive singular. Fem. nouns are, in all cases of the singular, like the nominative.

Dieser Mann ist der Bruder des Gärtners. Diese Frau ist die Schwester des Schuhmachers. Dieses Kind ist der Sohn des Schneiders. Die Magd des Nachbars ist die Nichte des Schreiners. Wir haben den Palast des Königs gesehen. Die Mutter der Königin ist angekommen. Mein Vater hat den Garten der Tante gekauft. Die Schwester der Nachbarin ist noch sehr jung. Die Freundin des Dichters ist sehr liebenswürdig. Die Fenster dieses Hauses sind zu groß. Die Häuser dieser Stadt sind sehr schön. Die Kinder dieser Frau sind alle krank. Unsere Gärten sind hübscher, als die Gärten des Arztes. Unsere Mutter ist älter, als die Mutter dieses Kindes. Dieser Hund gehört dem Sohne des Nachbars. Diese kleine Katze gehört dem Kinde der Nachbarin.

80.

der Kaufmann, the merchant.

OBSERVATION.—1) ein, mein, dein &c. have in the genitive singular the same terminations as the definite article: eines, einer, eines &c. 2) Adjectives preceded by one of the determinative words der, dieser, mein &c. have in the genitive singular the termination en.

Dieser Knabe ist der Sohn eines Kaufmanns. Diese Dame ist die Tochter eines Arztes. Karl ist der Freund meines Bruders. Emilie ist die Freundin meiner Schwester. Das Haus unseres Nachbars ist größer, als das unsrige. Die Kinder unserer Taute sind sehr fleißig. Karl hat die Federn seines Bruders und seiner Schwester genommen. Elise hat die Nadeln ihrer Freundin verloren. Die Straßen euerer Stadt sind breiter, als die Straßen unserer Stadt. Die Fenster eueres Hauses sind zu hoch. Wir haben den letzten Brief deiner Mutter gelesen. Mein Vater hat den Garten deines Onkels gekauft. Wo ist der Fingerhut meiner kleinen Schwester? Wo ist der Regenschirm meines Bruders? Hier sind die Bücher deines Vaters und die Bänder deiner Mutter. Louise hat für das Kind ihrer Schwester einen hübschen Vogel gekauft.

81.

The books of my father are more useful than yours [1]. The gardener of my uncle is a very skillful man. The sister of my aunt has arrived. The garden of your neighbor is very pretty. Who has bought the house of the physician? Who has taken the stick of my friend? Have you seen the palace of the king and queen? The father of our maid-servant is very poor. Henry has lost the pens of his brother and sister. We have found the little dog of your friend. Emily has found the ribbons of your (female) friend. The child of this poor woman is ill. Lewis is the son of a physician, and Mathilda is the daughter of a rich merchant.

82.

von, of, from, by.

von der Mutter, from the mother.

von dem Kinde, from the child.

von dem Vater, from the father.

von meinem Bruder, from my brother.

von diesem Buche, from this book.

von wem, from whom?

der Krieg, the war; der Handel, the commerce; gehorsam, obedient.

ich spreche, I speak; wir sprechen, we speak; wird geliebt, is loved.

the brother of this child, der Bruder dieses Kindes.

we speak of this child, wir sprechen von diesem Kinde.

Das ist das Buch meines Bruders. Ich habe dieses Buch von meinem Bruder erhalten. Das sind die Nadeln meiner Schwester. Ich habe diese Nadeln von meiner Schwester erhalten. Von wem hast du diese Blumen erhalten? Ich habe diese Blumen von dem Gärtner erhalten. Von wem habt ihr diesen Garten gekauft? Wir haben diesen Garten von dem Bruder unseres Onkels gekauft. Ich spreche von unserem König und (von) unserer Königin. Wir sprechen von dem Kriege und dem Handel. Heinrich ist ein gehorsamer Sohn; er wird von seinem Vater und seiner Mutter geliebt. Elise ist ein liebenswürdiges Kind, sie wird von ihrem Onkel und ihrer Taute geliebt. Unſer Kutſcher hat einen Brief von ſeinem Sohne und ſeiner Tochter erhalten. Das ſind die Schuhe dieſes armen Mädchens; es hat dieſe Schuhe von einem reichen Kaufmanne erhalten.

83.

I have seen the palace of the king and queen. We speak of the king and queen. That is not the dog of our neighbor. I have not received this dog from our neighbor. From whom have you bought this beautiful horse? We have bought this beautiful horse from the brother of my uncle. I have received these ribbons from the sister of my (female) friend. I speak of my son and daughter. Charles is very obedient; he is loved by his uncle and aunt. Mathilda is very amiable; she is loved by her father and mother.

84.

das Brot, the bread;
das Fleiſch, the meat;
der Apfel, the apple;
der Kaffee, the coffee.
die Milch, the milk.
das Waſſer, the water.
der Wein, the wine.
die Suppe, the soup.
das Gemüſe, the vegetables.

Brot, (some) bread.
Fleiſch, (some) meat.
Aepfel, (some) apples.
der Bleiſtift, the pencil.
die Taſſe, the cup.
der Buchhändler, the bookseller.
er verkauft, he sells.
gegeſſen, eaten.
getrunken, drunk, taken.

Ich habe Kaffee und Milch getrunken. Du hast Wasser und Wein getruuken. Mein Bruder hat Brot und Fleisch, Suppe und Gemüse gegessen. Wir haben Kirschen und Pflaumen gekauft. Dieser Buchhändler verkauft Bücher, Federu, Dinte und Bleistifte. Der Schuhmacher macht Schuhe und Stiefel. Der Schreiner macht Tische und Stühle. Unser Nachbar hat Vögel, Hunde, Pferde und Katzen. Euere Taute hat Messer und Gabeln, Tassen und Gläser gekauft. Wir haben in Loudou Löwen und Tiger gesehen. Wir sind den ganzen Tag beschäftigt gewesen; wir haben Briefe geschrieben und Aufgaben gemacht.

85.

was, what?

Have you [1] drunk wine or beer? I have drunk neither wine nor beer, but I have drunk some coffee and milk. What have you [1] eaten? I have eaten some meat, vegetables and bread. What have you [1] bought? I have bought some paper and pens. What have you done, my children? We have done some exercises and written some letters. Henry has received shoes and stockings. Emily and Mathilda have received some ribbons, rings and flowers. We have sold houses and gardens. Have you [1] already seen (any) swallows this year? Yes, my dear, I bave already seen many swallows.

86.

viel, much, many.	mehr, more.
wie viel, how much?	genug, enough.
so viel, so much, as much.	der Pfeffer, the pepper.
zu viel, too much.	das Salz, the salt.
wenig, little, few.	der Senf, the mustard.
weniger, less, fewer.	das Geld, the money.

das Obst, fruit; es gibt, es sind, there is, there are; gebet mir, give me.

Gebet mir ein wenig Fleisch. Ich habe genug Brot. Du hast zu viel Salz und Pfeffer. Wilhelm hat viel Geld; er hat mehr Geld, als ich. Wir haben weniger Obst, als ihr. Louise hat weniger Federu, als Mathilde. Karl hat mehr Aufgaben gemacht, als Ludwig. Hast du so viel Geld, wie meiu Bruder? Ein armer Mann hat wenig Freunde. Gebet dem Kinde ein wenig Milch. Mein Bruder hat zu viel Wein getrunken. Diese Mutter hat viele Kinder. Wie viel Hunde hat deiu Vater? Es gibt dieses Jahr wenig Kirschen, aber viel Pflaumen. Mein Freund hat diese Woche mehr Briefe erhalten, als ich. Ich habe zu wenig Diute. Ich habe genug Papier.

87.

Our gardener has many trees and flowers. I have eaten a little meat and vegetables. Have you got mustard enough? I have enough salt and pepper. Your neighbor has much money; he is a very

rich man. Give a little wine to this poor woman.
This gentleman has few friends, but he has many
horses and dogs. Have you (got) as many apples and
pears as we? We have not so many as you, but we
have more cherries and plums · than you. What
have you [1] drunk, Henry? I have taken a little
wine, and Lewis has taken some beer. We have
eaten many cherries.

88.

das Pfund, the pound.	der Korb, the basket.
die Elle, the ell, the yard.	die Halsbinde, the cravat.
das Paar, the pair.	der Handschuh, the glove.
das Stück, the piece.	die Leinwand, the linen.
das Dutzend, the dozen.	der Käse, the cheese

geschickt, sent.

zwei Pfund Köse, two pounds of cheese.
drei Paar Handschuhe, three pair of gloves.

OBSERVATION.—The words Pfund, Paar, Stück, Dutzend are generally invariable when preceded by a number.

Wir haben heute zwanzig Ellen Leinwand, sechs Hals-
binden und drei Paar Handschuhe erhalten. Mein Bruder
hat zwei Paar Schuhe und ein Paar Stiefel gekauft.
Unser Onkel hat dem alten Gärtner sechs Flaschen Wein
geschickt. Karl hat ein Glas Bier getrunken und ein
Stück Fleisch gegessen. Meine Mutter hat sechs Paar
Strümpfe und drei Pfund Kirschen gekauft. Ich habe von
dem Gärtner einen Korb Blumen erhalten. Gebet dieser

armen Frau ein Glas Waſſer und ein Stück Brod und
Käſe. Dieſes Kind hat zu viel Salz und Senf. (Die)
kleine Louiſe hat zu viel Obſt gegeſſen.

89.

hungrig, hungry; durſtig, thirsty.
gib mir, give me.

I am hungry, give me a piece of meat and a
little bread. Are you [1] not thirsty? Yes, I am
very thirsty. There is a bottle of beer. What
have you drunk at Mrs. Bender's? We have taken
two glasses of wine. Give this poor child a glass
of water and some bread and cheese. My aunt has
bought four cravats, six pair of gloves and a dozen
pair of stockings. The shoemaker has made a pair
of shoes for Louisa and two pair of boots for William.
How many ells of linen have you bought? I have
bought twelve ells. Ferdinand has bought a pound
of plums, six pounds of coffee and two dozen knives
and forks. Henry is very naughty; he has drunk
too much wine. William has drunk one glass of
beer.

90.

Wilhelm, William.	Mathilde, Mathilda.
Wilhelm's, of William.	Mathildens, of Mathilda.
Wilhelm, dem Wilhelm, } to William.	Mathilden, der Mathilde, } to Mathilda.

Johann, John.   Köln, Cologne.
Karoline, Caroline.   Aachen, Aix-la-Chapelle.
Lüttich, Liege.

er heißt, he is called, his name is; wohnt, lives.

Dieser Knabe heißt Johann, und seine Schwester heißt Karoline. Der Vater Wilhelm's ist angekommen. Die Mutter Louisens ist ausgegangen. Ludwig's Onkel ist sehr reich. Heinrich's Tante ist sehr krank. Mathildens Schwestern sind sehr liebenswürdige Mädchen. Karolinens Bruder ist ein hübscher Knabe. Von wem hast du diese Blumen erhalten? Ich habe diese Blumen von Heinrich und Ferdinand erhalten. Wem hast du deine Vögel gegeben? Ich habe meine Vögel Karl und Louisen gegeben. Wohnt dein Onkel in Köln oder in Aachen? Mein Onkel wohnt in Paris. Ist dein Freund von Straßburg oder von Metz? Er ist weder von Straßburg noch von Metz; er ist von Lüttich.

91.

What is the name of your son? His name is John, and his little brother is called Alfred. What is the name of your (female) friend? She is called Pauline. Are you [1] the brother of Charles and William? I am Henry's and John's brother. Mathilda's bonnet is finer than Louisa's. To whom have you given your birds? We have given our birds to John and Ferdinand. From whom have you [1] received this pretty bouquet? I have received this pretty bouquet from Emily. My uncle lives at Cologne, and my nephew at Aix-la-Chapelle.

92.

Nom. and acc. plur.	Gen. plur.	Dat. plur.
die,	der,	den.
diese,	dieser,	diesen.
meine,	meiner,	meinen.
euere,	euerer,	euern.

ihr (referring to a female noun in the singular), her.

ihr (referring to several nouns or a noun in the plural), their.

OBSERVATION.—1) All nouns take **n** in the dative plural; the other cases of the plural are like the nominative. 2) Adjectives preceded by one of the determinative words die, diese, meine, deine &c. have in all cases of the plural the termination **en**.

Gebet diesen armen Kindern Brot. Der Handel der Engländer ist groß. Der Vater dieser Mädchen ist ein berühmter Künstler. Ich spreche von den Dichtern der Deutschen. Die Blätter dieser Bäume sind alle verwelkt. Die Häuser euerer Nachbarn sind so hoch, wie das eurige. Diese Pferde gehören meinen Brüdern. Diese Ringe gehören meinen Schwestern. Die artigen und gehorsamen Kinder werden von ihren Vätern und Müttern geliebt. Ich habe meine alten Kleider den Mägden gegeben. Wir sprechen von unseren neuen Klei-n und Hüten. . Wer hat meinen Töchtern diese hübschen Sträuße geschickt? Hast du heute Briefe von deinen Freunden erhalten? Wir sind in Köln und in Aachen gewesen; wir haben die großen Kirchen dieser Städte gesehen. Diese Dame hat ihren Söhnen zwei Dutzend Paar Strümpfe und ihren Nichten ein Dutzend Paar Handschuhe geschickt. Gebet meinen Kindern ihre Bücher; sie haben ihre Aufgaben noch nicht gemacht.

THIRD PART.

COLLECTION OF WORDS.

1. Die Familie, the family.

die Eltern, the parents
der Vater, the father
die Mutter, the mother
der Sohn, the son
die Tochter, the daughter
der Bruder, the brother
die Schwester, the sister
der Großvater, the grand-
father
die Großmutter, the grand-
mother
ein Enkel, a grandson
eine Enkelin, a granddaugh-
ter
der Onkel, the uncle
die Tante, the aunt
der Neffe, the nephew

die Nichte, the niece
der Vetter, the cousin
die Cousine, the fem. cousin
ein Stiefvater, a step-father
der Pathe, the god-father
die Pathin, the god-mother
ein Knabe, a boy
ein Mädchen, a girl
der Mann, }
der Gemahl, } the husband
die Frau, }
die Gemahlin, } the wife
ein Wittwer, a widower
eine Wittwe, a widow
eine Waise, an orphan
der Vormund, the guardian
das Mündel, the ward

2. Das Haus, the house.

die Thür, the door
das Schloß, the lock
der Schlüssel, the key
die Klingel, the bell
der Riegel, the bolt
das Stockwerk, the story
die Treppe, the staircase
eine Stufe, a step
ein Zimmer, a room
ein Saal, a drawing-room
das Besuchzimmer, the parlor
ein Schlafzimmer, a bedroom
der Balcon, the balcony
ein Fenster, a window
eine Scheibe, a pane
die Fensterladen, the shutters
die Decke, the ceiling
der Fußboden, the floor

der Kamin, the chimney
die Küche, the kitchen
der Heerd, the hearth
der Speicher, the garret
das Dach, the roof
ein Ziegel, a tile
der Hof, the yard
der Stall, the stable
die Krippe, the manger
der Holzschuppen, the wood-
house
die Scheune, the barn
der Wagenschuppen, the
coach-house
der Keller, the cellar
der Garten, the garden
das Treibhaus, the green-
house

3. Möbel, furniture.

der Tisch, the table
der Stuhl, the chair
der Sessel, the arm-chair
das Kanapee, the sofa
die Standuhr, the clock
der Spiegel, the looking-
glass

das Gemälde, the painting
der Kupferstich, the engrav-
ing
der Schrank, the press
die Schublade, the drawer
die Kommode, the bureau,
the chest of drawers

Schaukelstuhl, rocking-chair
das Bett, the bed
die Wiege, the cradle
die Decke, the blanket
das Leintuch, the sheet
die Matratze, the mattress
das Kissen, the pillow, the cushion
der Vorhang, the curtain
der Teppich, the carpet
der Ofen, the stove
der Topf, the pot
die Schachtel, the box
die Schüssel, the dish
der Teller, the plate
der Krug, the pitcher
der Leuchter, the candlestick
eine Kerze, a candle
eine Lampe, a lamp
der Löffel, the spoon
die Gabel, the fork
das Messer, the knife

die Tasse, the cup
die Untertasse, the saucer
das Tischtuch, the table-cloth
die Serviette, the napkin
das Handtuch, the towel
das Glas, the glass, the tumbler
die Flasche, the bottle
der Kork, the cork
der Becher, the mug
die Zuckerdose, the sugar-bowl
der Senftopf, the mustard-pot
das Salzfaß, the salt-cellar
die Lichtscheere, the snuffers
Zündhölzchen, matches
das Stocheisen, the poker
die Feuerzange, the tongs
der Korb, the basket
eine Schaufel, a shovel

4. Kleidung, clothing.

der Rock, the coat
der Mantel, the cloak
der Ueberzieher, the overcoat
das Futter, the lining

die Tasche, the pocket
die Knöpfe, the buttons
das Knopfloch, the button-hole

eine Jacke, a jacket

eine Weste, a waistcoat

die Hose, the pantaloons

die Unterhose, the drawers

die Mütze, the cap

der Hut, the hat, bonnet

die Halsbinde, the cravat

eine Haube, a cap

der Kamm, the comb

der Ohrring, the ear-ring

das Halsband, the necklace

das Halstuch, the neck-tie

der Schleier, the veil

das Kleid, the dress, gown

eine Schürze, an apron

das Band, the ribbon

der Gürtel, the girdle

das Armband, the bracelet

der Handschuh, the glove

der Ring, the ring

eine Broche, a brooch

eine Uhr, a watch

das Zifferblatt, the dial

die Zeiger, the hands

der Strumpf, the stocking

das Strumpfband, the garter

die Socke, the sock

der Stiefel, the boot

der Schuh, the shoe

der Pantoffel, the slipper

das Hemd, the shirt

der Spazierstock, the cane

das Taschentuch, the pocket handkerchief

die Bürste, the brush

die Brille, the spectacles

eine Lorgnette, an eye-glass

eine Stecknadel, a pin

eine Nähnadel, a needle

der Regenschirm, the umbrella

der Sonnenschirm, the parasol

die Börse, the purse

5. Nahrungsmittel, victuals.

das Brot, the bread

Schwarzbrot, brown bread

Weißbrot, white bread

das Mehl, the meal, flour

das Fleisch, the meat

der Braten, the roast meat

Kalbfleisch, veal

Rindfleisch, beef

Hammelfleisch, mutton

Speck, bacon

der Schinken, the ham

das Gemüse, vegetables

die Brühe, the sauce

die Suppe, the soup

das Ei, the egg

der Eierkuchen, the omelet

die Torte, the tart, pie.

der Salat, the salad

der Senf, the mustard

das Salz, the salt

das Oel, the oil

der Essig, the vinegar

der Pfeffer, the pepper

die Butter, the butter

der Käse, the cheese

der Kuchen, the cake

das Obst, fruit

das Frühstück, breakfast

das Mittagessen, dinner

das Abendessen, supper

der Hunger, hunger

der Durst, thirst

das Wasser, the water

der Wein, the wine

das Bier, the beer

der Kaffee, the coffee

die Milch, the milk

die Chocolade, chocolate

der Branntwein, brandy

der Thee, the tea

6. Der menschliche Körper, the human body.

der Mensch, man

der Körper, the body

der Kopf, the head

das Haar, the hair

das Gesicht, the face

die Stirn, the forehead

die Augenbrauen, the eye-
brows

das Auge, the eye

das Augenlid, the eyelid

die Wimper, the eyelash

der Augapfel, the eyeball

die Nase, the nose

das Nasenloch, the nostril

das Ohr, the ear

das Kinn, the chin

der Bart, the beard

die Wange, the cheek

der Mund, the mouth

die Lippe, the lip

ein Zahn, a tooth

das Zahnfleisch, the gums

die Zunge, the tongue

der Hals, the neck

die Kehle, the throat

die Schulter, the shoulder

der Rücken, the back

der Arm, the arm

der Ellbogen, the elbow

die Faust, the fist

die Hand, the hand

der Finger, the finger

der Daumen, the thumb

der Nagel, the nail

der Magen, the stomach

die Brust, the breast

der Bauch, the belly

das Herz, the heart

die Seite, the side

das Knie, the knee

das Bein, the leg

der Fuß, the foot

die Ferse, the heel

die Haut, the skin

der Knochen, the bone

das Blut, the blood

der Schweiß, the perspiration

die Nerven, the nerves

die Adern, the veins

7. Die Stadt, the town.

eine Stadt, a town, city

eine Vorstadt, a suburb

die Hauptstadt, the capital

das Zollhaus, the custom-house

die Brücke, the bridge

der Graben, the ditch

der Wall, the rampart

die Mauer, the wall

der Glockenthurm, the steeple

der Thurm, the tower

die Festung, the fortress

die Straße, the street

das Pflaster, the pavement

der Marktplatz, the market-place

der Brunnen, the fountain, the well

das Rathhaus, the city-hall

die Post, the post-office

das Theater, the theater

das Zeughaus, the arsenal
das Spital, the hospital
die Kirche, the church
die Domkirche, the cathedral
ein Kloster, a convent
eine Schule, a school
das Gefängniß, the prison
die Börse, the exchange

der Kaufladen, the store
der Palast, the palace
der Gasthof, the hotel
die Schenke, the tavern
die Herberge, the inn
die Umgegend, the environs
der Kirchhof, the church-
    yard, cemetery

8. Das Land, the country.

das Land, the country
ein Bauer, a peasant
ein Berg, a mountain
ein Thal, a valley
ein Hügel, a hill
ein Bauernhaus, a cottage
ein Dorf, a village
ein Weiler, a hamlet
ein Schloß, a castle
ein Meierhof, a farm
der Pächter, the farmer
eine Mühle, a mill
ein Mühlrad, a mill-wheel
der Wald, the forest, wood
der Busch, the grove
ein Fußpfad, a path
der Weg, the way, the road
die Landstraße, the highway

das Feld, the field
eine Quelle, a spring
ein Bach, a brook
der Mist, the dung
der Staub, the dust
eine Wiese, a meadow
der Baumgarten, the or-
    chard
das Korn, the grain
der Weizen, the wheat
der Roggen, the rye
die Gerste, the barley
der Hafer, the oats
das Stroh, the straw
die Aehre, the ear
der Halm, the blade
der Pflug, the plough
die Egge, the harrow

das Heu, the hay
die Heugabel, the fork
eine Sense, a scythe
die Ernte, the harvest

ein Schnitter, a reaper
eine Garbe, a sheaf
eine Sichel, a sickle
der Dreschflegel, the flail

9. Die Schule, the school.

die Schule, the school
der Schüler, the school-boy, scholar
der Lehrer, the teacher
der Zögling, the pupil
ein Pult, a desk
das Buch, the book
der Einband, the binding
das Blatt, the leaf
eine Seite, a page
das Wort, the word
eine Silbe, a syllable
der Buchstabe, the letter
die Grammatik, the grammar
die Dinte, the ink
das Dintenfaß, the inkstand
die Schrift, the writing
das Schreibheft, the copy-book
das Zeichenbuch, the draw-ing-book
das Papier, the paper

der Bogen, the sheet
die Feder, the pen, quill
das Federmesser, the pen-knife
das Löschblatt, the blotting-paper
der Streusand, the pounce
der Bleistift, the pencil
das Lineal, the ruler
eine Zeile, a line
der Dintenfleck, the blot
der Schwamm, the sponge
eine Schiefertafel, a slate
der Griffel, the slate-pen-cil
eine Aufgabe, an exercise
eine Uebersetzung, a trans-lation
das Beispiel, the example
der Fehler, the mistake
eine Lection, a lesson
die Prüfung, examination

10. Künste und Gewerbe, arts and trades.

ein Gewerbe, a trade
ein Handwerk, a profession
ein Bäcker, a baker
ein Müller, a miller
ein Metzger, a butcher
ein Bierbrauer, a brewer
ein Schneider, a tailor
ein Schuster, a shoemaker
ein Schmied, a smith
ein Hufschmied, a black-
smith
ein Sattler, a saddler
ein Schreiner, a joiner
ein Zimmermann, a carpen-
ter
ein Goldarbeiter, a gold-
smith
ein Uhrmacher, a watch-
maker
ein Maurer, a mason
ein Böttcher, a cooper

ein Kaminfeger, a chimney-
sweeper
ein Kupferschmied, a copper-
smith
ein Gerber, a tanner
ein Seiler, a rope-maker
ein Barbier, a barber
ein Künstler, an artist
ein Buchdrucker, a printer
Buchhändler, bookseller
Buchbinder, bookbinder
ein Baumeister, an architect
ein Schauspieler, an actor
ein Musiker, a musician
ein Arzt, a physician
ein Wundarzt, a surgeon
ein Zahnarzt, a dentist
ein Apotheker, an apothecary
ein Wirth, an innkeeper
ein Gärtner, a gardener
ein Maler, a painter

11. Vierfüßige Thiere, quadrupeds.

das Thier, the animal
das Pferd, the horse
das Füllen, the colt
der Esel, the ass

der Maulesel, the mule
der Hund, the dog
die Katze, the cat
die Ratte, the rat

die Maus, the mouse
das Kaninchen, the rabbit
das Wiesel, the weasel
der Maulwurf, the mole
der Ochs, the ox
der Stier, the bull
die Kuh, the cow
das Kalb, the calf
das Schaf, the sheep
das Lamm, the lamb
das Schwein, the hog
die Ziege, the goat
die Gemse, the chamois
der Hase, the hare

das Eichhorn, the squirrel
der Affe, the monkey
der Biber, the beaver
der Hirsch, the deer
das Reh, the roe
der Fuchs, the fox
der Dachs, the badger
der Wolf, the wolf
der Bär, the bear
der Löwe, the lion
der Tiger, the tiger
der Elephant, the elephant
das Kameel, the camel
der Leopard, the leopard

12. Vögel, birds.

der Vogel, the bird
der Hahn, the cock, rooster
die Henne, the hen
das Huhn, the chicken
der Truthahn, the turkey
der Schwan, the swan
die Gans, the goose
die Ente, the duck
die Taube, the pigeon
der Pfau, the peacock
die Wachtel, the quail
die Schnepfe, the snipe

die Amsel, the blackbird
die Lerche, the lark
die Nachtigall, the nightingale
der Kanarienvogel, the canary-bird
der Finke, the chaffinch
der Hänfling, the linnet
die Meise, the titmouse
das Rothkehlchen, the redbreast
die Schwalbe, the swallow

der Sperling, the sparrow
die Elster, the magpie
der Rabe, the raven
die Krähe, the crow
die Eule, the owl
der Kuckuk, the cuckoo
der Zeisig, the siskin

der Papagei, the parrot
der Sperber, the hawk
der Falke, the falcon
der Storch, the stork
der Strauß, the ostrich
der Adler, the eagle
der Geier, the vulture

13. Fische und Insecten, fishes and insects.

der Fisch, the fish
der Hecht, the pike
der Karpfen, the carp
der Aal, the eel
die Forelle, the trout
der Häring, the herring
der Krebs, the lobster
die Schildkröte, the tortoise
der Walfisch, the whale
die Schlange, the snake
die Eidechse, the lizard
die Kröte, the toad
der Frosch, the frog
der Wurm, the worm
die Raupe, the caterpillar

die Schnecke, the snail
das Insect, the insect
der Käfer, the beetle
die Spinne, the spider
die Milbe, the mite
die Motte, the moth
der Floh, the flea
die Fliege, the fly
die Mücke, the gnat
die Biene, the bee
der Blutegel, the leech
die Wespe, the wasp
die Grille, the cricket
die Heuschrecke, the locust
Schmetterling, butterfly

14. Bäume und Blumen, trees and flowers.

der Baum, the tree
der Strauch, the shrub

der Ast, the branch
der Zweig, the twig

die Wurzel, the root

die Rinde, the bark

das Blatt, the leaf

der Apfel, the apple

der Apfelbaum, the apple-
tree

die Birne, the pear

der Birnbaum, the pear-tree

die Pflaume, the plum

der Pflaumenbaum, the plum-
tree

die Kirsche, the cherry

der Kirschbaum, the cherry-
tree

die Aprikose, the apricot

die Pfirsich, the peach

die Nuß, the nut

die Himbeere, the raspberry

die Johannisbeere, the cur-
rant

die Stachelbeere, the goose-
berry

die Erdbeere, the strawberry

die Kastanie, the chestnut

die Eiche, the oak

die Tanne, the pine

die Linde, the linden

die Buche, the beech

die Birke, the birch

die Weide, the willow

die Pappel, the poplar

die Blume, the flower

der Stengel, the stalk

der Dorn, the thorn

die Rose, the rose

der Rosenstock, the rose-bush

eine Knospe, a bud

eine Nelke, a pink

eine Tulpe, a tulip

eine Lilie, a lily

eine Levkoje, a gilly-flower

das Veilchen, the violet

das Gänseblümchen, the
daisy

die Maiblume, the lily of
the valley

die Kornblume, the corn-
flower

die Hyacinthe, the hyacinth

die Sonnenblume, the sun-
flower

die Flieder, the lilac

der Blumenstrauß, the bouquet

der Blumentopf, the flower-
pot

15. Die Zeit, the time.

die Zeit, the time	Juni, June
der Augenblick, the moment	Juli, July
die Minute, the minute	August, August
die Stunde, the hour	September, September
der Tag, the day	October, October
ein Festtag, a holiday	November, November
ein Werktag, a working day	December, December
der Morgen, the morning	die Woche, the week
Mittag, noon	Montag, Monday
Nachmittag, afternoon	Dienstag, Tuesday
der Abend, the evening	Mittwoch, Wednesday
die Nacht, the night	Donnerstag, Thursday
Mitternacht, midnight	Freitag, Friday
das Jahr, the year	Samstag, Saturday
der Monat, the month	Sonntag, Sunday
Januar, January	die Jahreszeit, the season
Februar, February	der Frühling, spring
März, March	der Sommer, summer
April, April	der Herbst, autumn
Mai, May	der Winter, winter

16. Krankheiten und Gebrechen, diseases and defects.

die Krankheit, the illness	die Masern, the measles
das Arzneimittel, the remedy	die Blattern, the small-pox
eine Pille, a pill	das Fieber, the fever
der Husten, the cough	die Heiserkeit, hoarseness
der Schlucken, the hiccough	die Ohnmacht, the swooning

eine Erkältung, a cold

die Kolik, the colic

eine Geschwulst, a swelling

eine Wunde a wound

eine Narbe, a scar

der Schnupfen, the cold

die Schwindsucht, the consumption

die Gicht, the gout

die Gelbsucht, the jaundice

ein Hühnerauge, a corn

ein Stammler, a stammerer

ein Stummer, a mute

ein Buckliger, a hunchback

ein Blinder, a blind man

17. Vermögen der Seele, faculties of the soul.

die Seele, the soul

der Geist, the mind

die Vernunft, the reason

der Gedanke, the thought

das Gedächtniß, the memory

der Wille, the will

die Liebe, love

der Haß, hatred

die Furcht, fear

die Hoffnung, hope

die Scham, shame

die Wahrheit, truth

eine Lüge, a lie

der Verdruß, anger

der Zorn, wrath

der Streit, the quarrel

eine Beleidigung, an injury

die Freude, joy

das Vergnügen, pleasure

die Traurigkeit, sadness

der Neid, envy

das Mitleid, pity

die Güte, kindness

die Freundschaft, friendship

die Tugend, virtue

die Weisheit, wisdom

das Laster, vice

der Geiz, covetousness

der Stolz, pride

der Müßiggang, idleness

die Faulheit, laziness

die Verachtung, scorn

die Bosheit, wickedness

die Grausamkeit, cruelty

die Frömmigkeit, piety

die Geduld, patience

die Bescheidenheit, modesty | der Muth, courage
die Ehre, honor | die Hochachtung, esteem
das Gewissen, conscience | die Treue, fidelity
der Ruhm, glory | die Schmeichelei, flattery

18. Eigennamen, proper names.

Abele, Adeline | Jakob, James
Alexander, Alexander | Johann, John
Amalie, Amelia | Joseph, Joseph
Anton, Anthony | Julie, Julia
Albert, Albert | Julius, Julius
Alfred, Alfred | Karl, Charles
Christian, Christian | Karoline, Caroline
Elise, Eliza | Katharine, Catherine
Emilie, Emily | Klara, Clara
Eduard, Edward | Laura, Laura
Franz, Francis | Lucia, Lucy
Franziska, Frances | Ludwig, Lewis
Friedrich, Frederic | Margarethe, Margaret
Gottfried, Godfrey | Maria, Mary
Georg, George | Matthäus, Matthew
Hannchen, Jane | Peter, Peter
Heinrich, Henry | Therese, Theresa
Henriette, Henrietta | Wilhelm, William
Helene, Helen | Wilhelmine, Wilhelmina

Specimens of German Writing.

1.

Wie heißt du, mein Sohn? Ich heiße
Ernst. Wie heißt deine Schwester?
Sie heißt Bertha. Bist du älter, als
deine Schwester? Meine Schwester ist
älter; sie ist zwölf Jahren, und ich bin
zehn Jahre alt. Hast du nicht einen
Onkel in Paris? Ja, der älteste Bruder meiner Mutter wohnt in Paris.
Hat er Kinder? Er hat einen Sohn
und zwei Töchter gehabt; er hat alle
seine Kinder verloren.

2.

New York und Philadelphia sind große
Städte. Die größten Städte von Europa
sind London und Paris. Ist Paris
größer, als London? Nein, London
ist größer. Bist du in London gewesen?

Nein, mein Vater und meine Mutter sind drei Wochen da gewesen. Haben sie die Königin gesehen? Nein, sie haben die Königin nicht gesehen.

3.

Unsere Katze hat eine Maus. Wir haben viele Mäuse und Ratten in unserem Hause; ich habe heute eine Ratte in meinem Zimmer gesehen. Wir haben Suppe, Gemüse, Fleisch, Brot und Kirschen gegessen und eine Tasse Kaffee getrunken. Der Tischler hat ein Dutzend Stühle und zwei Tische gemacht. Ich bin hungrig und durstig; gebt mir ein Stück Käse und Brot und ein Glas Bier! Meine Schwester hat von unserem Nachbar, dem Gärtner, zwei Sträuße und einen schönen Korb Blumen erhalten.

4.

Diese Kinder sind krank; sie haben zu viel Obst gegessen. Wir haben von unserem Vater Geld erhalten und haben Birnen und Pflaumen gekauft. Warum habt ihr nicht ein nützliches Buch gekauft? Dieses kleine Mädchen hat ihre Nadeln und ihren Fingerhut in meinem Zimmer verloren. Ist das dein Regenschirm, Carl? Nein, er gehört meiner Schwester; ich habe den meinigen meinem Freunde Heinrich geliehen.

5.

Hast du den letzten Brief unseres Vaters gelesen, Louise? Ja, ich habe auch schon zwei Briefe, einen unserem Vater und einen unserer Schwester Caroline geschrieben. Haben wir heute den neunten August? Nein, wir haben den ersten. Gib mir ein wenig Papier, ich habe nicht genug. Unser Onkel hat viel Unglück gehabt; er hat alle seine Häuser und Gärten verkauft und sein ganzes Vermögen verloren.

6.

Warum seid ihr heute nicht in der Schule, Kinder? Heute ist der vierte Juli. Ist euer Vater ausgegangen? Ja, er ist sehr beschäftigt; er ist den ganzen Tag nicht hier gewesen. Wem gehört dieser schöne Garten? Er gehört unserem Onkel. Habt ihr viele Blumen in dem Garten? Wir haben viele Tulpen und schöne Rosen. Gebt mir eine Rose. Hier ist eine. Gib diese hübsche weiße Rose meiner lieben Freundin Emilie.

7.

Dieser Kaufmann verkauft Tassen
und Gläser, Messer und Gabeln, Bücher
und Papier, Federn und Tinte, Schuhe und
Strümpfe, Bänder und Leinwand. Hast
du einer gekauft? Ja, ich habe fünf
Dutzend für einen Thaler erhalten.
Haben die Deutschen große Dichter?
Ja, die berühmtesten Dichter der Deutschen sind Göthe und Schiller. Seid ihr
fleißig gewesen, Kinder? Ja, Vater,
wir sind sehr fleißig gewesen; wir sind
den ganzen Tag nicht ausgegangen und
haben alle unsere Aufgaben gemacht.
Wir haben der Mutter unsere Aufgaben gezeigt.

THE ALPHABET.

𝔄	a		𝔍	j		𝔖	ſ	
A	a		J	j		S	s	ß
𝔅	b		𝔎	k			s	ss
B	b		K	k				
ℭ	c		𝔏	l		𝔖𝔱		
C	c		L	l		St		
𝔇	d		𝔐	m		𝔗	t	
D	d		M	m		T	t	
𝔈	e		𝔑	n		𝔘	u	
E	e		N	n		U	u	
𝔉	f		𝔒	o		𝔙	v	
F	f		O	o		V	v	
𝔊	g		𝔓	p		𝔚	w	
G	g		P	p		W	w	
ℌ	h		𝔔	q		𝔛	r	
H	h		Q	q		X	x	
	or		ℜ	r		𝔜	y	
			R	r		Y	y	
ℑ	i					ℨ	z	
I	i					Z	z	

MODIFIED VOWELS.

𝔄̈ ä | ä | 𝔒̈ ö | ö | 𝔘̈ ü | ü

1. der *der*, die *die*, das *das*, der Vater *Vater*
Vater, die Mutter *die Mütter*, das Buch
das Buch, der Garten the garden *der Garten*
die Stadt the town the city *die Stadt*, und *und*.

2. der Sohn the son *der Sohn*, die Tochter the daughter *die*
Tochter, das Haus the house *das Haus*, der Tisch the table
der Tisch, die Feder the pen *die Feder*, das Papier the paper
das Papier.

3. der Mann the man *der Mann*, die Frau the woman *die*
Frau, das Kind the child *das Kind*, der Hund the dog *der*
Hund, die Katze the cat *die Katze*, das Pferd the horse
das Pferd.

4. der Bruder the brother *der Bruder*, die Schwester the sister *die*
Schwester, das Dorf the village *das Dorf*, der Vogel the bird

der Vogel,   die Blume   *die Blume,*
the flower

das Schloß   *das Schloß.*
the castle

6. ein (masc.)   eine (fem.)   ein (neuter)
   a, an   *ein,*   a, an   *eine,*   a, an

ein.   ein Vater   *ein Vater,*   eine Mutter   *eine*
a father   a mother

Mutter,   ein Buch   *ein Buch.*
a book

9. mein (masc.)   meine (fem.)
   my   *meine,*   my   *meine,*

mein (neuter)   dein (masc.)   deine (fem.)
my   *mein.*   your (thy)   *dein,*   your (thy)

deine,   dein (neuter)   *dein,*   der Onkel   der Onkel,
your (thy)   the uncle

die Tante   *die Tante,*   das Glas   *das Glas,*
the aunt   the glass

der Freund   *der Freund,*   die Flasche   *die Fla-*
the friend   the bottle

sche,   das Wasser   *das Wasser.*
the water

10. unser   *unser,*   unsere   *unsere,*   unser   *unser,*
    our   our   our

euer   *euer,*   euere   *euere,*   euer   *euer.*   unser Vater
your   your   your   our father

unser Vater,   unsere Mutter   *unsere*
our mother

Mutter,   unser Haus   *unser Haus.*
our house

dein Vater
euer Vater
your father

deine Mutter
euere Mutter
your mother

dein Haus
euer Haus
your house

12. dieser
this

diese
this

dieses
this

dieser Vater
this father

diese Mutter
this mother

dieses Kind
this child

14. alt
old

jung
young

neu
new

gut
goo

treu
faithful

müde
tired

groß great,
large, tall

klein little,
small, short

schön
beautiful
fine

krank
ill
sick

nützlich
useful

fleißig
diligent

Karl
Charles

Louise
Louisa

ist
is

16. nicht
not

reich
rich

arm
poor

für
for

17. sind
are

19. artig
good, gentle *artig*, glücklich
happy *glücklich*.

20. der Arzt
the physician *der Arzt*, Heinrich
Henry *Heinrich*,

die Magd
the maid-servant *die Magd*, Emilie
Emily

Emilie, Herr
gentleman, sir *Herr*, hier ist
here is *hier ist*,

da ist
there is *da ist*, wo
where *wo*.

22. ich bin
I am *ich bin*, du bist
you are (thou art) *du bist*,

der Neffe
the nephew *der Neffe*, die Nichte
the niece *die Nichte*,

munter
gay *munter*, zufrieden
contented *zufrieden*, immer
always

immer, sehr
very *sehr*, ja
yes *ja*, nein
no *nein*.

24. er, sie, es ist
he, she, it is *er*, *sie*, *es ist*, traurig
sad *traurig*,

traurig, aber
but *aber*, auch
also *auch*, hier
here *hier*, da
there *da*.

26. wir sind
we are *wir sind*, ihr seid
you are *ihr seid*, sie
they

sind
are *sie sind*, oder
or *oder*, noch
still *noch*.

28. der gute Vater
the good father *der gute Vater*, die
the

gute Mutter
good mother *die gute Mutter*, das gute
the good

Kind
child _[handwritten: Das gute Kind,]_ geschickt
skilful _[handwritten: geschickt,]_

falsch
false _[handwritten: falsch.]_

30. blind
blind _[handwritten: blind.]_

32. scharf
sharp _[handwritten: scharf,]_ lieb
dear _[handwritten: lieb.]_

33. der Gärtner
the gardener _[handwritten: Der Gärtner,]_ schon
already _[handwritten: schon.]_

35. der erste
the first _[handwritten: Der ersten,]_ der zweite
the second _[handwritten: Der zweiten,]_

der dritte
the third _[handwritten: Der dritten,]_ der vierte
the fourth _[handwritten: Der vierten,]_

der fünfte
the fifth _[handwritten: Der fünften,]_ der sechste
the sixth _[handwritten: Der sechsten,]_

der siebente
the seventh _[handwritten: Der siebenten,]_ der achte
the eighth _[handwritten: Der achten,]_

der neunte
the ninth _[handwritten: Der neunten,]_ der zehnte
the tenth _[handwritten: Der zehnten,]_

der elfte
the eleventh _[handwritten: Der elften,]_ der zwölfte
the twelfth _[handwritten: Der zwölften,]_

der letzte
the last _[handwritten: Der letzten,]_ Juni
June _[handwritten: Juni,]_ Juli
July _[handwritten: Juli;]_

August
August _[handwritten: August,]_ Ludwig
Lewis _[handwritten: Ludwig,]_ Wilhelm
William

[handwritten: Wilhelm,] Paul
Paul _[handwritten: Paul,]_ Franz
Francis _[handwritten: Franz,]_

Katharine
Catherine _[handwritten: Katharine,]_ Pauline
Pauline _[handwritten: Pauline,]_

bescheiden *(handwritten)* unartig *(handwritten)* heute
modest naughty to-day

(handwritten) morgen *(handwritten)* übermorgen
to-morrow the day after to-

der erste Auguſt *(handwritten)*
morrow *(handwritten)* the first *of* August

der vierte Juli
(handwritten) the fourth *of* July *(handwritten)*

37. klein *(handwritten)* kleiner *(handwritten)* alt *(handwritten)*
small smaller old

älter *(handwritten)* groß *(handwritten)* größer *(handwritten)*
older large larger

nützlich *(handwritten)* nützlicher *(handwritten)* die
useful more useful the

Erde *(handwritten)* die Sonne *(handwritten)* der
earth the sun the

Rhein *(handwritten)* die Donau *(handwritten)*
Rhine the Danube

ſtark *(handwritten)* breit *(handwritten)* als *(handwritten)*
strong broad than

39. der meinige *(handwritten)* der deinige *(handwritten)*
mine yours (thine)

(handwritten) der unſrige *(handwritten)* der eurige
ours yours

(handwritten) der Ring *(handwritten)* die Uhr
the ring the watch

die Uhr, das ist *[das ist]* nicht so....als
that is   not so....as

nicht so....als, so....wie *[so....wie]*
                 as....as

41. klein *[klein]* kleiner *[kleiner]* der kleinste
small   smaller   the smallest

der kleinste. *[der kleinste]* alt *[alt]* älter *[älter]*
               old   older

der älteste *[der älteste]* groß *[groß]* größer
the oldest   large   larger

größer, *[größer]* der größte *[der größte]* nützlich
                   the largest   useful

nützlich, *[nützlich]* nützlicher *[nützlicher]* der nütz-
                       more useful   the most

lichste *[lichste]* das Metall *[das Metall]*
useful   the metal

das Metall, *[das Metall]* das Eisen *[das Eisen]* das Silber
                           the iron   the silver

das Silber, *[das Silber]* das Thier *[das Thier]* Friedrich
                           the animal   Frederic

Friedrich, *[Friedrich]* Mathilde *[Mathilde]* Elise
                         Mathilda   Elisa

Elise, *[Elise]* die Aufgabe *[die Aufgabe]* leicht
                 the exercise   easy

leicht, *[leicht]* unglücklich *[unglücklich]*
                   unhappy

43. sein, seine, sein *[sein, seine, sein]* ihr, ihre, ihr
his   her

ihr, ihre, ihr. *[ihr, ihre, ihr]* die Dame *[die Dame]*
                                    the lady

die Freundin
the friend (female) *(script)*,   der Kutscher
the coachman

(script)

45. Singular.   Plural.

der Tisch
the table *(script)*,   die Tische
the tables *(script)*.

der Stuhl
the chair *(script)*,   die Stühle
the chairs *(script)*.

die Stadt
the town *(script)*,   die Städte
the towns *(script)*.

die Nacht
the night *(script)*, der Hut
the hat, bonnet *(script)*,

der Strumpf
the stocking *(script)*,   der Brief
the letter *(script)*

die Hand
the hand *(script)*,   der Zahn
the tooth *(script)*

der Fuß
the foot *(script)*,   der Schuh
the shoe *(script)*

die Maus
the mouse *(script)*.

46. kurz
short *(script)*,   rein
clean *(script)*,   weiß
white *(script)*.

warm
warm *(script)*,   gestern
yesterday *(script)*, jetzt
now *(script)*,

Paris
Paris *(script)*,   London
London *(script)*,   das sind
these are

(script).

48. das Kleid
the dress, gown *[handwriting]*   das Band
        the ribbon

[handwriting]   das Glas *[handwriting]*   das Haus
     the glass   the house

[handwriting] das Buch *[handwriting]* das Kind
     the book   the child

[handwriting] das Ei *[handwriting]* das Schloß *[handwriting]*
     the egg   the castle

[handwriting] das Dorf *[handwriting]* das Loch
     the village   the hole

[handwriting] das Blatt *[handwriting]* der Wurm
     the leaf   the worm

[handwriting] der Wald
     the forest, wood *[handwriting]*

der Mann
the man *[handwriting]*

49. hoch *[handwriting]* schmutzig *[handwriting]* häßlich
   high   dirty   ugly

[handwriting] verwelkt *[handwriting]* grün
     withered   green

[handwriting] nicht mehr *[handwriting]* alle *[handwriting]*
     no more   all

noch nicht
not yet *[handwriting]*

51. der Schneider *[handwriting]* der Schuhmacher
   the tailor   thc shoemaker

[handwriting] der Italiener *[handwriting]*
     the Italian

[handwriting] der Engländer *[handwriting]*
     the Englishman

das Fenster
the window *das Fenster*,

das Zimmer
the room *das Zimmer*,

der Spiegel
the mirror *der Spiegel*,

der Stiefel
boot *der Stiefel*,

der Löffel
the spoon *der Löffel*,

die Gabel
the fork *die Gabel*,

die Nadel
the needle *die Nadel*,

das Mädchen
the girl *das Mädchen*,

faul
lazy *faul*,

zu
too *zu*.

53. der Löwe
the lion *der Löwe*,

der Hase
the hare *der Hase*,

die Ratte
the rat *die Ratte*,

der Knabe
the boy *der Knabe*,

die Kirche
the church *die Kirche*,

die Schule
the school *die Schule*,

der Russe
the Russian *der Russe*,

der Franzose
the Frenchman *der Franzose*,

der Deutsche
the German *der Deutsche*,

der Preuße
the Prussian *der Preuße*,

die Pflaume
the plum *die Pflaume*,

die Straße
the street *die Straße*,

der Apfel
apple *der Apfel*,

der Tiger
the tiger *der Tiger*,

furchtſam
timid, afraid *[handwriting]*,

liebenswürdig *[handwriting]*
amiable

[handwriting],

tapfer
brave *[handwriting]*,

beſſer
better *[handwriting]*.

55. die Stunde
the hour *[handwriting]*,

die Schwalbe
the swallow *[handwriting]*

[handwriting],

die Kirſche
the cherry *[handwriting]*,

angenehm
pleasant, agreeable *[handwriting]*.

56. die Ente
the duck *[handwriting]*,

die Roſe
the rose *[handwriting]*,

die Gans
the goose *[handwriting]*,

die Tulpe
the tulip *[handwriting]*,

die Frucht
the fruit *[handwriting]*,

Herr N.
Mr. N. *[handwriting]*.

58. ich habe
I have *[handwriting]*,

du haſt
you have (thou hast) *[handwriting]*,

er hat
he has *[handwriting]*,

wir haben
we have *[handwriting]*,

ihr habt
you have *[handwriting]*,

ſie haben
they have *[handwriting]*,

die
the

Dinte
ink *[handwriting]*.

59. ich habe das Meſſer nicht
I have not the knife,
I have not got the knife *[handwriting]*

60. der Dichter   der Nachbar
the poet   the neighbor

der Künstler
the artist

berühmt   viel   viele
famous   much   many

wer?
who?

61. weder....noch   ich habe
neither....nor   I have

weder das Brod noch das Fleisch
neither the bread nor the meat

62. gekauft   verkauft
bought   sold

gesehen   verloren   gefunden
seen   lost   found

genommen
taken

warum?
why?

64. der seinige   der ihrige
his   hers

gesucht   hübsch
looked for   pretty

66. eins   zwei   drei   vier
one   two   three   four

fünf   sechs   sieben
five   six   seven

acht eight *aust,* neun nine *nnnn,* zehn ten *zuhn,* elf eleven *nlf,*

zwölf twelve *zwölf,* dreizehn thirteen *drnizuhn,* vierzehn fourteen

vinrzuhn, fünfzehn fifteen *funfzuhn,* sechzehn sixteen *puf-*

zuhn, siebzehn seventeen *sinbzuhn,* achtzehn eighteen *aust-*

zuhn, neunzehn nineteen *nnunzuhn,* zwanzig twenty *zwan-*

zig. das Jahr the year *das Jahr,* der Monat the month *dnr*

Monat, die Woche the week *din Wuhn,* der Tag the day

Dnr Day, wie alt? how old? *win alt?*

68. der Vater the father *dnr Vatnr,* den Vater the father *dnn*

Vatnr. dieser Mann this man *dinfnr Mann,* diesen this

Mann man *dinfnn Mann.* erhalten received *nufaltnn,*

geschrieben written *gnfhruibnn,* gelesen read *gnlnfnn.* der the

Stock stick, cane *dnr Nort,* der König the king *dnr König,*

die Königin the queen *din Königin,* oft often *oft.*

69. ein Garten a garden *nnn Gartnn,* einen Garten a garden *nnnn*

mein Hund
my dog *(script)*, my

Hund
dog *(script)*.

70. der Schreiner
the joiner *(script)*, die Birne
the pear *(script)*

(script), gebracht
brought *(script)*.

71. das Glück
the happiness, good luck *(script)*, das
the

Unglück
misfortune *(script)*, das Vergnügen
the pleasure *(script)*

(script), das Geschäft
the business *(script)*

(script), das Vermögen
the fortune *(script)*

ehemals
formerly *(script)*, gehabt
had *(script)*, gemacht
made, done

(script).

72. beschäftigt
busy, occupied *(script)*.

73. gewesen
been *(script)*, angekommen
arrived *(script)*

ausgegangen
(script), gone out *(script)*, ich bin gewesen
I have been

(script), er ist angekommen
he has arrived *(script)*

(script), sie sind ausgegangen
they have gone out *(script)*

ganz *ganz,* den ganzen Tag
ausgegangen, whole, all *ganz,* the whole day,

all day *den ganzen Tag,* wie lange? *wie*
lange? in *in,* Frau N. *Frau N.,* bei
how long? in in, Mrs. N. at

Frau N.
Mrs. N. *bei Frau N.*

74. Kopfweh *Kopfweh,* der Strauß
headache the nosegay, bouquet

der Strauß.

75. der, die, das *der, die, das,* dem, der, dem
the to the

dem, der, dem. der Vater *der Vater,*
die Mutter *die Mutter,* das Kind *das Kind.*
the mother the child

dem Vater *dem Vater,* der Mutter *der*
to the father to the mother

Mutter, dem Kinde *dem Kinde.* es
to the child it

gehört
belongs *es gehört,* sie gehören *sie gehören,*
they belong

versprochen
promised *versprochen,* geliehen *geliehen,*
lent

gegeben
given *gegeben,* gezeigt *gezeigt.*
shown

76. der Fingerhut *[handwritten]* der Regenſchirm
    the thimble the umbrella

der Thaler *[handwritten]*
the (German) dollar

77. das Brot *[handwritten]* gebet *[handwritten]*
    the bread give

78. wem? *[handwritten]*
    to whom?

79. der, die, das *[handwritten]* des, der, des *[handwritten]*
    the . of the

[handwritten] der Vater *[handwritten]* die Mutter
the father the mother

[handwritten] das Kind *[handwritten]* des
the child of

Vaters *[handwritten]* der Mutter
the father of the mother *[handwritten]*

[handwritten] des Kindes *[handwritten]* die
of the child the

Nachbarin *[handwritten]* der Palaſt
neighbor (female) the palace

[handwritten]

80. der Kaufmann *[handwritten]*
    the merchant

82. von von der Mutter
    of, from, by *[handwritten]* from the mother *[handwritten]*

[handwritten] von dem Kinde
from the child *[handwritten]*

von dem Vater *[handwritten]* von meinem
from the father from my

Bruder *von meinem Bruder,* von diesem
brother from this

Buche *von diesem Buche,* von wem?
book from whom? *von*

wem? der Krieg *der Krieg,* der Handel
the war the commerce

der Handel, gehorsam *gehorsam,* ich spreche
obedient I speak

ich spreche, wir sprechen *wir sprechen,*
we speak

wird geliebt *wird geliebt,* der Bruder dieses Kindes
is loved the brother of this child

der Bruder dieses Kindes, wir
we

sprechen von diesem Kinde *wir sprechen von die-*
speak of this child

sem Kinde.

84. das Brot *das Brot,* Brot *Brot,*
the bread (some) bread

das Fleisch *das Fleisch,* Fleisch *Fleisch,*
the meat (some) meat

der Apfel *der Apfel,* Aepfel *Aepfel,*
the apple (some) apples

der Kaffee *der Kaffee,* die Milch *die Milch,*
the coffee the milk

das Wasser *das Wasser,* der Wein *der Wein,*
the water the wine

die Suppe *die Suppe,* das Gemüse *das Ge-*
the soup the vegetables

der Bleiftift
the pencil   die Taffe
the cup

der Buchhändler
the bookseller

er verkauft
he sells   gegeſſen
eaten

getrunken
drunk, taken

85. was?
what?

86. viel
much, many   wie viel?
how much?

fo viel
so much, as much   zu viel
too much

wenig
little, few   weniger
less, fewer   mehr
more

genug
enough   der Pfeffer
the pepper

das Salz
the salt   der Senf
the mustard

das Geld
the money   das Obft
the fruit

es gibt, es ſind
there is, there are

gebet mir
give me

88. das Pfund
the pound   die Elle
the ell, yard

das Paar
the pair   das Stück
the piece

das Dutzend *[das Dutzend]* der Korb
the dozen the basket

der Korb, die Halsbinde *[die Halsbinde]*
the cravat

der Handschuh *[der Handschuh]* die Leinwand
the glove the linen

die Leinwand, der Käse *[der Käse]* geschickt
the cheese sent

geschickt, zwei Pfund Käse zwei
two pounds of cheese

Pfund Käse, drei Paar Handschuhe den
three pair of gloves

Paar Handschuhe.

89. hungrig *[hungrig]* durstig *[durstig]* gib mir
hungry thirsty give me

gib mir.

90. Wilhelm *[Wilhelm]* Wilhelm's *[Wil-]*
William of William

helm's, Wilhelm, dem Wilhelm *[Wilhelm]*
to William

den Wilhelm, Mathilde *[Mathilde]*
Mathilda

Mathilden's *[Mathilden]* Mathilden, der Mathilde
of Mathilda to Mathilda

Mathilden, den Mathild, Johann
John

Johann, Karoline *[Karoline]* Köln
Caroline Cologne

Köln, | Aachen Aix-la-Chapelle | Lüttich Liege

er, heißt he is called, his name is | wohnt lives

92. die | der | den | diese
the | of the | to the | these

dieser | diesen | meine
of these | to these | my

meiner | meinen | euere
of my | to my | your

euerer | euern | ihr | ihr
of your | to your | her | their

READING EXERCISES.

(The Notes to these Exercises contain only those words and grammatical constructions not found in the *Rudiments.*)

---

1. Häuser, Dörfer, Städte.

(Die) Menschen können[1] nicht immer im Freien[2] leben[3]; deshalb[4] bauen[5] sie Häuser. (Die) meisten[6] Häuser sind von Holz[7] oder Stein gemacht. Ein Haus hat eine Thür und Fenster (plur.). Durch[8] die Thür gehen[9] wir ein[10] und aus[11]; durch die Fenster erhalten[12] wir Luft[13] und Licht[14]. Die Thür ist von Holz gemacht; die Fenster aber sind von Holz und Glas gemacht. Das Haus hat ein oder mehr(ere) Stockwerke. In dem Hause gibt es große und kleine Zimmer; sie heißen: Küche, Schlafzimmer, Wohnzimmer, Speisezimmer. In einem Dorfe gehört zu (den) meisten Häusern auch ein Garten. In dem Garten gibt es Früchte, Blumen und nützliche Gemüse. Eine große Anzahl[15] von Häusern bildet[16] eine Stadt. In jedem[17] Lande gibt es eine Stadt, welche[18] Hauptstadt heißt. So ist London die Hauptstadt von England. Die Hauptstadt der Vereinigten Staaten[19] ist Washington; allein (aber) die größte Stadt in den Vereinigten Staaten ist New York. Die Häuser und Straßen in all unseren großen Städten sind mit[20] Gas beleuchtet[21]. Nur[22] in sehr kleinen Städten und Dörfern sind die Straßen des (at) Nachts ganz dunkel[23]. Die Straßen der Städte haben ein

Pflaster von Stein oder Holz; an (on) jeder Seite der Straße ist ein Fußpfad, auf dem²⁴ die Leute²⁵ gehen²⁶.

¹can. ²in the open air. ³live. ⁴hence. ⁵build. ⁶most. ⁷wood. ⁸by. ⁹go. ¹⁰in. ¹¹out. ¹²receive. ¹³air. ¹⁴light. ¹⁵number. ¹⁶forms. •¹⁷each. ¹⁸which. ¹⁹of the United States. ²⁰with. ²¹lighted. ²²only. ²³quite dark. ²⁴on which. ²⁵people. ²⁶walk.

2. Unsere Bedürfnisse¹

Alle Männer, Frauen und Kinder bedürfen² Nahrung³, Wohnung⁴, Kleidung und Unterricht⁵. Der Landmann⁶, der Bäcker, der Gärtner, der Müller, der Metzger versehen uns⁷ mit Nahrung. Der Schneider, der Schuster, der Hutmacher, der Gerber machen⁸ unsere Kleidung; der Baumeister, der Maurer, der Zimmermann, der Schreiner, der Maler sind beschäftigt mit unsern Wohnungen. Außerdem⁹ haben wir Schüler noch viele andere¹⁰ Bedürfnisse. Wir bedürfen² Lehrer, die¹¹ uns unterrichten¹², nützliche Bücher zum¹³ Lesen¹⁴, eine Schiefertafel und einen Griffel, Feder und Dinte, Schreibhefte und Zeichenbücher zum Schreiben¹⁵ und Zeichnen¹⁶. Wir haben alle diese Dinge von unseren lieben Eltern erhalten und wir wollen¹⁷ ihnen¹⁸ immer dankbar¹⁹ sein¹⁷.

¹wants. ²need. ³food. ⁴lodging. ⁵instruction. ⁶farmer. ⁷versehen uns, provide us. ⁸make. ⁹besides. ¹⁰other. ¹¹who. ¹²instruct us. ¹³for. ¹⁴reading. ¹⁵writing. ¹⁶drawing. ¹⁷wir wollen sein, we will be. ¹⁸to them. ¹⁹grateful.

3. Der Herr¹ und der Diener².

Ein reicher Engländer war³ auf Reisen⁴ und kam⁵ mit seinem Diener in⁶ einen Gasthof, wo sie die Nacht über⁷ blieben⁸. (Den) nächsten⁹ Morgen verlangte¹⁰ der Herr seine Stiefel und der Diener brachte sie¹¹ bald nachher¹². Was¹³ ist das, Thomas? sagte¹⁴ der Herr, meine Stiefel sind nicht rein! Nein, (mein) Herr, antwortete¹⁵ Thomas, der Weg ist sehr schmutzig und Ihre Stiefel würden¹⁶ (doch) bald wieder¹⁷ schmutzig sein. Du hast Recht¹⁸, sagte der Herr; wo sind die Pferde? Aber — ich habe mein Frühstück noch nicht gehabt, antwortete Thomas. Keine Geschichten¹⁹, sagte der Herr, du würdest²⁰ (doch) bald wieder hungrig sein.

¹master. ²servant. ³was. ⁴on a journey. ⁵came. ⁶to. ⁷die Nacht über, over night. ⁸remained. ⁹next. ¹⁰demanded. ¹¹brought them. ¹²soon afterwards. ¹³translate: wie. ¹⁴said. ¹⁵replied. ¹⁶würden sein, would be. ¹⁷again. ¹⁸you are right. ¹⁹no matter. ²⁰du würdest sein, you would be.

4. Muth.

Ein Schiff¹ war in einem schrecklichen² Sturme³ in großer Gefahr⁴. Ein kleiner Knabe, der⁵ auch auf (on) dem Schiffe war, blieb⁶ so zufrieden und heiter wie gewöhnlich⁷. Ein Matrose⁸ fragte ihn⁹: Bist du nicht furchtsam in diesem schrecklichen Sturme? Was sollte ich fürchten¹⁰? antwortete der Knabe, mein Vater ist an dem Steuerruder¹¹.

¹ship. ²awful. ³storm. ⁴danger. ⁵who. ⁶remained. ⁷usual. ⁸sailor. ⁹asked him. ¹⁰should I fear. ¹¹the helm.

5. Der Schwertfisch[1].

Der Schwertfisch heißt so von der Form[2] der Nase, welche[3] wie[4] ein Schwert gestaltet[5] ist. Die ganze Länge[6] des Schwertfisches ist ungefähr[7] zwanzig (20) Fuß. Der Körper hat fast[8] keine[9] Schuppen[10] und sieht aus[11], wie der Körper einer Makrele. Er (it) schwimmt[12] mit großer Schnelligkeit[13], hat eine außerordentliche[14] Stärke[15] und ist deshalb[16] der Schrecken[17] für alle Fische. Das Fleisch des Schwertfisches dient (ist gut) zur (for) Nahrung. Er (it) wird fast in allen Meeren gefunden und mit der Harpune gefangen[18].

[1]sword-fish. [2]form. [3]which. [4]like. [5]shaped. [6]length. [7]about. [8]almost. [9]no. [10]scales. [11]looks. [12]swims. [13]swiftness. [14]extraordinary. [15]strength. [16]therefore. [17]terror. [18]taken.

6. Das Pferd.

Das Pferd ist ein Hausthier[1]. Der Kopf ist länglich[2], die Ohren sind spitz[3]. An dem Halse hat das Pferd lange Haare, welche[4] Mähne[5] heißen. Der Schweif[6] des Pferdes ist lang und herabwallend[7]; an jedem Fuße hat es nur einen Huf[8]. Das Pferd ist ein schönes, muthiges[9] und starkes Thier. Gras, Klee[10], Heu und Hafer sind seine (its) Nahrung. Das Pferd ist dem Menschen sehr nützlich. Es wird zum (for) Reiten[11] und Ziehen[12] benutzt[13]. Aus (von) der Haut wird Leder[14] gemacht. Die Sattler und die Polsterer[15] gebrauchen[16] die Haare des Schweifes und der Mähne. Es gibt schwarze, weiße, braune[17] und graue[18] Pferde. Ein junges Pferd heißt Füllen[19]. Ein Füllen ist ein munteres Thier.

[1]domestic animal. [2]longish. [3]pointed. [4]which. [5]mane. [6]tail. [7]flowing. [8]hoof. [9]spirited. [10]clover. [11]riding. [12]drawing. [13]used. [14]leather. [15]upholsterers. [16]use. [17]brown. [18]gray. [19]colt.

7. Die Wallnuß[1]

(Der) kleine Georg hatte[2] in dem Garten seines Onkels eine Wallnuß gefunden, welche[3] noch in der grünen Schale[4] war. Der Knabe glaubte[5], er hätte[2] einen Apfel gefunden und versuchte[6] sie (it) zu essen[7]. Aber er warf[8] die Nuß bald weg und sagte: Pfui[9], wie bitter! Sein älterer Bruder Franz hob[10] die Nuß auf, schälte[11] sie (it) mit seinen Zähnen und sagte: Ich achte[12] diese bittere Schale nicht, weil[13] ich weiß[14]: da ist eine süße Frucht in einer bitteren Schale.

[1]the walnut. [2]had. [3]which. [4]shell. [5]believed. [6]tried. [7]to eat. [8]warf weg, threw away. [9]fie. [10]hob auf, took up. [11]peeled. [12]ich achte nicht, I don't mind. [13]because. [14]I know.

8. Der kluge[1] Staar[2].

Ein durstiger Staar fand[3] eine Flasche mit (of) Wasser und versuchte zu trinken[4]; allein (aber) er konnte[5] mit seinem kleinen Schnabel[6] das Wasser nicht erreichen[7], denn[8] die Flasche war nur halbvoll[9]. Er wollte[10] ein Loch in das Glas picken[11]; aber es war zu dick. Da[12] versuchte er die Flasche umzuwerfen[13], doch (but) er war zu schwach[14]. Endlich[15] hatte er einen glücklichen Einfall[16]; er warf[17] kleine Steinchen[18] in die Flasche; dadurch[19] stieg[20] das Wasser und er konnte es mit seinem Schnabel erreichen.

[1]clever. [2]starling. [3]found. [4]drink. [5]could. [6]beak. [7]reach. [8]for. [9]half-full. [10]wished. [11]to peck. [12]then. [13]upset. [14]weak. [15]at last. [16]idea. [17]cast, [18]pebble. [19]whereby. [20]rose.

9. Das zerbrochene[1] Hufeisen[2].

Ein Bauer ging[3] mit seinem kleinen Sohne über (ein) Feld. Sieh[4], sprach der Vater, da ist ein zerbrochenes Hufeisen, heb' es auf[5] und stecke[6] es in die Tasche. O, sagte Thomas, das ist zu viel Mühe[7]. Der Vater hob[8] das Hufeisen auf und steckte[9] es in seine Tasche. Im nächsten Dorfe verkaufte[10] er es einem Hufschmied für drei Cents. Mit diesem Gelde kaufte[11] er Kirschen.

Sie gingen weiter[12]. Die Sonne war sehr warm; weit und breit[13] war kein Haus, kein Baum, kein Brunnen. Thomas war sehr durstig und konnte kaum[14] gehen[15]. Da ließ[16] der Vater eine Kirsche fallen Schnell[17] bückte[18] sich Thomas und hob[8] sie (it) auf. Nach[19] wenigen Schritten[20] ließ der Vater wieder eine Kirsche fallen und bald darauf wieder eine (another) und jedes Mal[21] hob der Sohn sie (it) auf. Der Vater aber sagte lächelnd[22]: Thomas, was war leichter, das Hufeisen aufzuheben[23] oder die Kirschen?

[1]broken. [2]horse-shoe. [3]was going. [4]look. [5]heb' auf, pick up. [6]put. [7]trouble. [8]hob auf, picked up. [9]put. [10]sold. [11]bought. [12]went farther. [13]far and wide. [14]scarcely. [15]walk. [16]ließ fallen, dropped. [17]quickly. [18]bückte sich, stooped down. [19]after. [20]steps. [21]time. [22]laughing. [23]to pick up.

10. Der Fuchs und der Rabe.

Ein Rabe hatte[1] ein Stück Fleisch gestohlen[2], flog[3] auf (to) einen hohen Baum und begann[4] es zu verzehren (essen). Der Fuchs sah[5] es und sprach: O Rabe, du bist ein schöner Vogel. Deine Federn[6] sind so glänzend[7] wie die Federn des Adlers und wenn deine Stimme auch so schön ist, (so) gehörst[8] du zu den schönsten Vögeln der Welt. Die Worte des Fuchses gefielen[9] dem (the) Raben und er öffnete[10] seinen Schnabel, um zu singen[11]. Natürlich[12] ließ er das Fleisch fallen, der Fuchs ergriff[13] es und lachte[14] über (at) den thörichten[15] Raben.

[1]had. [2]stolen. [3]flew. [4]began. [5]saw. [6]feathers. [7]bright. [8]belongest. [9]pleased. [10]opened. [11]um zu singen, in order to sing. [12]of course. [13]seized. [14]laughed. [15]foolish.

Wm. R. Hearst.

Residence

Nr°. Pine Str.

San

STEIGER'S German Series.

AHN'S *German Primer.* Edited by W. GRAUERT. (Printed in bold type, and containing much German Script.) New Edition (with Paradigms and Vocabulary. Boards $0.45.

AHN'S *German Reading Charts.* 25 Plates, with Hand-Book for Teachers. By Dr. P. HENN. (These Wall-Charts are printed in very large German type, with German Script letters expressly cut for the same.) $1.00.

The same. The 25 Plates mounted on 13 boards. $4.50.—Varnished $6.00.
  (AHN'S *German Reading Charts* may be advantageously used, as an introductory course of German Reading, Writing and Spelling, with any German Grammar.)

AHN'S *German Script Charts.* 4 Plates. (German Script of very large size, mounted on 4 boards, varnished; suitable for permanent display on the wall.) $1.25.

AHN'S *First German Book.* By Dr. P. HENN. (Exercises in Reading, Writing, Spelling, Translation, and Conversation. Printed in bold type, and containing a very large amount of German Script. Designed for the lowest two grades.) Boards $0.25.

AHN'S *Second German Book.* By Dr. P. HENN. (Exercises in Writing, Reading, Translation, and Conversation. Containing much German Script. A sequel to the *First German Book.* With Paradigms and Vocabularies of all German and English words occurring in both these books.) Boards $0.45.

  These two books together form:

AHN'S *Rudiments of the German Language.* By Dr. P. HENN. (With Vocabularies. Edition of 1873.) Boards $0.65.

Key to AHN'S *Rudiments of the German Language.* By Dr. P. HENN. Bds. $0.25.

AHN'S *Third German Book.* By Dr. P. HENN. (With Paradigms, Vocabularies, German Script, etc.) Boards $0.45

Key to AHN'S *Third German Book.* By Dr. P. HENN. Boards $0.25.

AHN'S *Fourth German Book.* By Dr. P. HENN. In press.

AHN'S *Rudiments of the German Language.* (Old Edition of 1870.) Boards $0 35.

AHN'S *Method of Learning the German Language.* Revised by GUSTAVUS FISCHER. (With German Script.) First Course, Boards $0 50. Second Course, Boards $0.50. Both together, Half Roan $1.00.

Key to AHN'S *Method* by G. FISCHER. Boards $0.30

AHN'S *New Practical and Easy Method of Learning the German Language.* With pronunciation by J. C. OEHLSCHLAEGER. Revised Edition. (With many Reading Exercises in German Script.) First Course (Practical Part), Boards $0 60; Second Course (Theoretical Part), Boards $0.40. Both together, Boards $1.00, Half Roan $1.25.

Key to AHN'S *Method* by J. C. OEHLSCHLAEGER. In press.

AHN'S *First German Reader.* With Notes by W. GRAUERT. (With much German Script.) Boards $0.50.—*Second German Reader.* With Notes and Vocabulary by W. GRAUERT. (With much German Script.) Boards $0.70.
  The two *Readers* bound together, Half Roan $1.20.

Key to AHN'S *First German Reader.* Boards $0.30.

Key to AHN'S *Second German Reader.* Boards $0.35.

AHN'S *German Handwriting* (all in German Script) A companion to every German Grammar and Reader. With Notes by W. GRAUERT. Boards $0.40.

AHN'S *Manual of German Conversation.* Revised by W. GRAUERT. Cloth $1.00.

AHN'S *German Letter-Writer.* In press.

GRAUERT'S *Manual of the German Language.* First Part, Boards $0.40; Second Part, Boards $0.40. Both together, Boards $0 70; Half Roan $0 90.

REFFELT'S *First Book for School and House.* (For instruction in Reading, Writing, Drawing and Arithmetic. In German. With Vocabulary of all German words. For use in American Schools.) Boards $0.30.

REFFELT'S *Second Book for School and House.* (In German. With Vocabulary of the German words in the first division of the Book. For use in American Schools.) Boards $0.50.

SCHLEGEL and **GRAUERT'S** *Course of the German Language.* Part First. *A German Grammar* for Beginners. By C. A. SCHLEGEL. Half Roan $1.25. Part Second. *A German Grammar* for advanced Pupils. By W.GRAUERT. In press.

SCHLEGEL'S *Series of Classical German Readers.* With Notes. Part First. *The First Classical German Reader.* With Notes and Vocabulary. By C. A. SCHLEGEL. Half Roan $1.00.—Part Second. *The Second Classical German Reader.* With Notes and Vocabulary. By C. A. SCHLEGEL. Half Roan $1.50.

E. Steiger, 22 & 24 Frankfort Str., New York.